Getting Horses Fit

CAROLYN HENDERSON

Getting Horses Fit

J.A. ALLEN · LONDON

ISBN-10: 0 85131 897 5
ISBN-13: 978 085131 897 4

J. A. Allen
Clerkenwell House
Clerkenwell Green
London ECIR OHT

J. A. Allen is an imprint of Robert Hale Limited

Edited by Martin Diggle
Design and typestting by Paul Saunders
Photographs by John Henderson, except for those on
page 143 and 145 by Kit Houghton
Line illustrations by Maggie Raynor

Printed by Kyodo Printing Co (S'pore) Pte Ltd, Singapore

Acknowledgements

Thanks to Caroline Burt and Martin Diggle for encouragement in the face of adversity and to all riders, horses and ponies who helped in so many ways. Special thanks go to my husband, John, not just for photography but for patience and help.

Contents

Introduction

FOR A HORSE TO PERFORM well – whether in eventing, endurance riding, showjumping, reining or any other of the myriad disciplines within the modern equestrian world – he has to be fit for the job. Fitness is essential whether you aim to compete at international level or local weekend competitions, because a fit horse will stand a better chance of staying sound, both physically and mentally, and will have a longer and more active life.

The same criterion applies if you choose not to compete but to ride purely for pleasure. The happy hacker or trail mount is still a working animal and needs to be prepared and maintained accordingly. After all, a Formula One racing car and a weekend runaround both need correct fuel and to be kept in good working order!

As every horse owner knows, the appliance of science underlines everything to do with the way we keep and look after our horses. Advances in diagnostic and applied veterinary medicine and nutrition allow a far greater understanding of the horse's physiological systems and vets can now spot potential problems much earlier than before. But, as most vets will acknowledge, a horse's best friend is an observant and aware owner, which is why intelligent as opposed to blinkered horsemastership is essential.

You are the one who has to decide whether your horse is too fat or too thin and to assess whether the fit of your saddle needs adjusting. You are the person who sees him every day and knows what is 'normal' for him, because that is the only way to spot when he might be feeling a little jaded or off colour. Specialists such as vets, farriers and saddle fitters can put right most problems, but owners have to identify them in the first place and as early as possible.

Driving trials Shetlands – all horses are athletes, whatever their size or job.

You are also the person who understands your horse's basic characteristics and temperament. This is important – for instance, if you have a naturally laid-back or even lazy horse, you need to know whether you need to push him a bit, or whether he is getting tired. A tired horse is just as prone to injury through, perhaps, stumbling or overreaching as one who is too full of himself.

That's why fitness is, first and foremost, your responsibility. It is not just a case of deciding that you want your horse to be able to, say, complete a 42 km (26 mile) ride in two months time and devising a week-by-week exercise chart. It demands a holistic approach, combining nutrition, management, exercise and schooling as well as a basic understanding of how a horse works, both physically and mentally. Getting a horse fit – or conditioning, if you prefer the term – means making sure that his cardio-vascular, muscular and skeletal systems are functioning efficiently and that he can cope mentally with all that is asked of him.

You have to be able to look at the big picture, as outlined in the previous paragraph, and to focus on the detail – which is why this book includes case histories of riders in different disciplines and circumstances and explains how they prepare their horses. Whilst they have different demands and criteria, they also have much in common. For a start, they all know and treat their horses as individuals and leave nothing to chance. They also adapt principles to their circumstances, whether of time constraints or geography.

Please do not fall into the trap of thinking that because, for example, you aim to do long pleasure rides it is only worth reading the section on endurance riding and that the other case histories will hold no interest. All the riders featured in this book have something to offer and you might find that their methods spark off ideas that could be applied to your horse. The modern horse world has been notorious for its tunnel vision – 'I don't do that because my horse is a dressage horse/show jumper/pleasure hack' – but over the past few years there have been signs that some enlightened people have started to break down the barriers. If everyone starts with the premise that 'my horse is an athlete' there is plenty to share.

Fitness can be a confusing subject, not least because there is no one way of doing things: as leading competition horse vet Andy Bathe points out, if you ask ten different event riders how they get their horses fit for a three-day event, you'll probably get ten different answers. It's like look-ing at a map; there might be only one destination, but there could be several ways of getting there, though all the routes will have common landmarks.

There are also many useful ways of keeping a horse in comfortable working order that can be used when you are getting him fit and whilst you are maintaining fitness. Some of these are dealt with later in this book and include everything from work you can do yourself, such as passive stretching exercises and long-reining, to those that necessitate calling in a qualified practitioner, such as equine muscle release therapy.

Because most riders have to fit in their horses around work and family commitments, the suggestions in this book are tailored accordingly. For instance, if you are a parent trying to get a pony who is too small for you to ride fit enough for a busy summer, there are suggestions to help. Similarly, the oft-quoted and perfectly true advice that hill work is a great asset in getting horses fit is not a lot of use if you live in a flat fenland area; again, there are alternative approaches.

This book is written with the amateur rider – who can still have professional standards – in mind. He or she may well want to participate in more than one activity and may be a keen Riding Club competitor – which definitely does not describe someone who bumbles around 'having a go' at everything cheerfully and not particularly well. Competition standards at this level have soared and many riders in club teams also compete successfully at affiliated level, or have raised their game and that of their horses to a standard whereby they could do, if they so wished. Therefore, the information and suggestions offered, especially regarding basic care and fitness, apply across a broad spectrum of disciplines. (Incidentally, although this book refers to riders, many of the fitness principles and approaches to it are equally applicable to driving; drivers can and do use approaches such as interval training.)

The first landmark in getting a horse fit is to understand what fitness actually means. Andy Bathe defines a fit horse as one who can do the job expected of him without undue stress, which makes sense whether you are talking about a high-goal polo pony or a novice endurance horse. Whilst fitness at top level becomes specialized – a Grade A showjumper would almost certainly not be able to complete a 160 km (100 mile) endurance ride without being overstressed, just as a human sprinter would not run a marathon – most of us take a more generalized approach to our riding and can get our horses to a stage of fitness at which they can take part in several activities at a reasonable level.

A lot of horses get fit enough for lower levels of competition more by accident than design, simply by doing their normal jobs. This can apply even up to Pre-novice eventing, the lower levels of affiliated showjumping and so on. But that does not mean you can assume your horse will become fit without you having to do anything about it; leaving it to chance is risky since every aspect of your horse's management, from nutrition to stable environment, plays a part. Equally, it is important to

FITNESS FACTS

The reason why different disciplines require different types of fitness is that they place different demands on an athlete, whether equine or human. You will often hear the terms aerobic and anaerobic exercise:

Aerobic exercise uses oxygen to generate energy and supports low or moderate intensity exercise over a prolonged period. Dressage, eventing and endurance riding are mainly aerobic activities.

Anaerobic metabolism takes place without oxygen. It supports periods of particularly demanding effort and is important in activities which have intermittent periods of high intensity exercise, such as polo and showjumping.

realize that, while a horse can be got fit to do a particular job, fitness in itself will not necessarily make him good at it. For instance, you can get a horse fit enough to compete at Novice level dressage, but if he is not balanced, supple and responsive enough, you are not going to score good marks.

This means that once you have established a basic level of fitness, you need to start incorporating work to make him more responsive and supple. More and more riders are realizing that they can borrow ideas and techniques from various disciplines to help in their own. Dubbed cross-training in the USA, this process can involve everything from hacking and perhaps doing a little pole or gridwork with the dressage horse to incorporating flatwork into the endurance animal or even the racehorse's routine so that he can bend equally on both reins. There is no better example of this than the National Hunt trainer Henrietta Knight, who came to racing from a background of all-round equitation and, in particular, eventing. She incorporates basic dressage into her charges' race preparation – and the results speak for themselves.

Just to make life even more complicated, it is also possible to get your horse too fit – though for most riders, this is admittedly a fairly small risk. Whilst it might seem better to have a horse too fit to complete, say, a Novice one-day event than not fit enough, you are inevitably putting miles on the clock and wear and tear on the engine all the time. When you move up through the competition gears, there is a risk that repeated stress will take its toll, especially on joints and tendons.

This caution has been applied particularly to top-level eventing. At one time, it was thought that horses needed a certain amount of actual competition to keep competition fitness, but the foot and mouth outbreak of 2001 made riders and researchers think again. The number of competitions was drastically reduced, but when horses did run again, it was found that most performed as well or even better.

Working out the ideal way of getting your horse fit will depend on several factors. These include his age and the amount of work he has done so far, the job you are aiming to get him fit for, his type or breed and even his conformation. No horse is perfect, but as we will see in Chapter 1, if a feature of conformation raises a hypothetical weakness, it is important to do everything possible to minimize the risk.

There are certain baselines that, it is generally agreed, apply no matter what the discipline. One is that a younger horse or one who has never been got fit before will take longer to reach the desired level than one who has. With young horses, you also have to take into account the fact that they are not physically mature and their systems may not be able to take the stress that a mature horse could cope with.

We often forget that whilst some horses might have reached physical maturity by the time they are around 5 years old, many do not. Breeds such as the Irish Draught, Warmbloods who do not have a high percentage of Thoroughbred blood and native ponies may not be fully mature until they are 7 or 8 years old.

If a horse has time off, either deliberately to give him a holiday or enforced by injury, the time it takes to get him back up to fitness will vary. It is now accepted that it is easier to reach previous fitness levels after a short break than a long one, which was why the traditional way of keeping hunters actually made little sense from a fitness perspective. The accepted method was to give them a summer at grass, bringing them up at the beginning of August and starting a three-month programme to get them ready for the opening meet, then turning them out at the end of the season.

More enlightened riders gradually decreased their hunters' work at the end of the season, then kept them on light work through the summer, which meant it was quite easy to make seamless progress into proper fitness training once again. Unfortunately, there were also plenty of horses who were hunting fit one day and turned out to grass the next, with nothing in between; letting down gradually, or 'de-training' as it has unfortunately become in modern parlance, is just as important to safeguard soundness.

We now know that it is never too early, or too late, to get a horse fit within his physical and mental limitations. For instance, whilst it has always been accepted that young horses need time and space to grow and develop physically and mentally, and that the best way to allow that is to give them as much time as possible outdoors, in recent years there have been some people who have taken the attitude that valuable youngsters should not be 'risked' in this way. They argue that keeping youngsters stabled for long periods or allowing them turnout in small areas, often alone to avoid the risk of them getting kicked, is acceptable and even advisable.

However, research has shown that mild stress helps develop healthy bone in growing youngsters. The keyword here is 'mild' – which translates as walking whilst grazing and indulging in the playful behaviour that comes naturally to all young animals, including children. There is also the vital question of mental as well as physical soundness: Professor Daniel Mills, Royal College of Veterinary Surgeons' recognized specialist in veterinary behavioural medicine, has reported that at least 3 per cent of the horses in the UK weave. With the horse population estimated conservatively at 500,000, that means that 15,000 carry out this repetitive behaviour – and restricted time outdoors and lack of social interaction are implicated factors.

At the other end of the age scale, whilst you can't expect to take a horse in his late teens who has led a sedentary life and get him fit enough to go round Badminton, an older horse who has maintained good levels of fitness and soundness can compete on equal and even better terms than younger animals. Matt Ryan's Kibah Tic Toc competed successfully at Badminton Horse Trials at the age of 18, Keeley Durham's Welham won the Hickstead Derby in his twenties and many top dressage horses reach their prime in their teens.

Another factor in the fitness conundrum that has become more widely appreciated in recent years is the fitness of the rider. At one time it was thought that we only needed to concentrate on the horse and, with a few exceptions – mainly in the field of eventing – most riders assumed that riding in itself was enough to get them fit. Whilst that may still work to some extent for some professionals who ride six or more horses a day, there is increased interest in ways to improve aspects of human fitness and suppleness, linked to nutrition.

For the majority of owners who have one or two horses and spend most of their day working away from them or with their families, rider fitness is an essential part of the jigsaw. A fit rider on a fit horse is a great combination. A fit rider can, to some extent, help a tired horse. But an unfit rider is a disaster waiting to happen, no matter what the status of his horse: if you are unfit, you will become tired and when you are tired, you are a dead weight which is out of balance.

For that reason, you will also find suggestions in these pages on how to improve your own fitness and reduce the risk of injury. Whether you enjoy the camaraderie of the gym or prefer a system that allows you to work alone, you can boost your fitness and, at the same time, your energy levels – thus enhancing the quality of your life all round. What more could you ask for?

1 Horses for courses

BEFORE YOU EMBARK on a fitness programme, it is a good idea to evaluate and keep a record of your horse's conformation, condition and state of health. This will enable you to identify any potential problem areas and hopefully tailor your management and work routines to make sure they do not become actual problems. At the same time, you will have a baseline to work from, so that as you progress, you can see how far you have come.

You also need to have definite but realistic aims. It does not matter whether they are grand or modest; whether your target is to compete eventually in a 160 km (100 miles) in one day endurance ride or a 24 km (15 mile) pleasure ride, a local riding club one-day event or international horse trials. It's important to draw the line between the achievable and the daydreams, because whether you are intending to work with the horse you already own or to buy one for a specific job, you will find various factors that influence your choice.

Most horses can compete successfully in most disciplines at lower to medium levels if they are correctly schooled, managed and ridden. Some go even further and break all the rules – there are lots of examples, such as native ponies succeeding in top-level endurance riding and 'ordinary' horses who excel in showjumping. But the demands of equestrian sports are far greater than those of even twenty years ago, so if you really are aiming at the top, it is very much a case of horses for courses.

To save potential heartbreak later on, you have to ask yourself two difficult questions. The first is: can I really expect my horse to cope with the demands I am going to put on him? And the second is, not surprisingly: if the answer is 'no', am I prepared to buy another who is? Only

Racing is one of the few activities that can be categorized as truly hard work.

A show horse who exemplifies good conformation and is in good condition for his job.

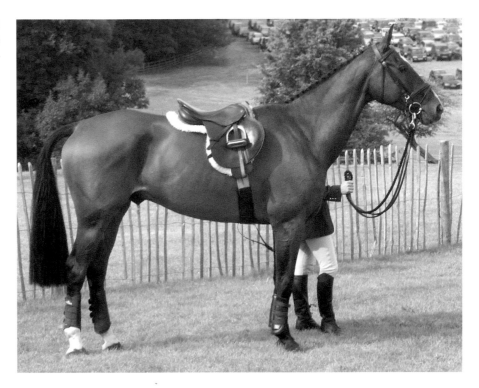

An advanced
event horse in
peak condition.

Most Lusitanos have
conformation that makes
collected work easier.

you know whether you would be happier staying with the horse you have and lowering your sights or looking for new horsepower to match your ambitions.

Conformation

Why evaluate conformation when it is the one thing about your horse that you can't change? For a start, the more you know about your horse and his potential strengths and weaknesses, the better equipped you are to get him fit for the job. Also, identifying the less-than-perfect areas – and there hasn't been a perfect horse born yet – will help you to lessen the risks of injury.

Whilst most people can learn to recognize good and bad points of conformation, the real art of assessing a horse lies in recognizing how plus and minus points complement or compound one another. For instance, a horse who is slightly long in the back and weak over the loins but has correct hind legs might still be a good prospect, but one who combines a weak back with weak hind legs could well see you running into problems.

If you are looking for a show horse, you are obviously looking for the nearest to perfection in terms of looks and action you can find and showing is a discipline all on its own. For all the other disciplines, you will be looking for a horse whose structure provides strength and efficiency, so you would not be so worried if, for instance, he was slightly shorter in the neck than ideal.

However, if he combines a short neck with an upright shoulder and pasterns, he will not be biomechanically efficient to take the concussion of true endurance riding or jumping at a high level. It's a bit like dominoes: one problem on its own might cause a bit of a wobble, but several in a row could well lead to collapse. So whilst the guidelines that follow are a good starting point, it's always best to involve a specialist eye. This could be either someone experienced and successful in the discipline you are aiming at, or a vet with specialist knowledge of it.

And if you're buying a horse to do a particular job, get him examined by a specialist horse vet who understands the demands of your discipline. Such people see a lot of problems, some that can be managed and some

Wulfstan Sioux City Soo, a pony who might not look a textbook dressage prospect, but one who has been successful in that discipline with rider Ebony Lawman

that can't, so don't begrudge them what might seem like a lot of money. It could save you a whole lot more in the long run, both financially and emotionally. Be realistic, because if you tell the examining vet that you want a horse to reach the top levels of eventing when you know that you will not get beyond Novice level, you may have a horse rejected as unsuitable who would do the job you really want him for perfectly.

A horse bought for a specific job should be examined by a vet with specialist knowledge of its demands.

Feet first

'No foot, no 'oss.' It's what the old horsemen used to say and is as true today as it was then; but as all good farriers will tell you, to get a true picture you need to look at the whole limb. However, starting from the ground up is the best way.

When you look at a horse's feet, the front ones should make one matching pair and the hind feet, another: look from behind as well as in front. Front feet should be rounded at the toe but hind feet are more oval; the

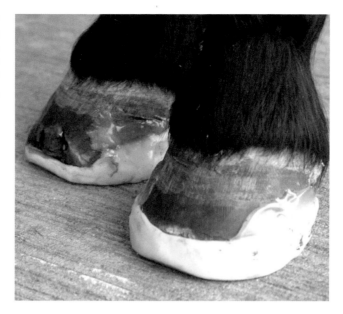

'No foot, no 'oss' – remedial shoes on a horse at the International League for the Protection of Horses.

reason for this is that when the horse stands naturally, his weight is distributed 60 per cent through the front feet and 40 per cent through the hind feet, so the front ones need a larger bearing area. The frogs should be well defined and the heels should be open, not contracted.

When you pick up a foot, the sole should be slightly concave. Flat soles are prone to corns and bruising; dropped soles, which are usually the result of chronic laminitis, are definitely to be avoided. Presumably your farrier is a good one who looks at each horse as an individual and takes care to keep the feet well balanced – if not, find a new one, because your farrier can be one of your greatest allies when it comes to getting your horse fit and keeping him sound.

Ideally, the feet should be of a size in keeping with the rest of the horse: you don't want to see a Thoroughbred with 'soup plates' or a heavyweight cob with little pony feet. Most people agree that of the two drawbacks, slightly small feet are a lesser evil than ones that are miles too big, as overlarge feet often lead to faulty movement and the risk of injury, especially from brushing.

Weak hoof walls usually mean brittle, crumbling feet. However, poor hoof quality can be linked to poor nutrition (see Chapter 3) and a balanced diet coupled, if necessary, with a good supplement may solve the problem. If in doubt, ask your farrier and/or vet's advice.

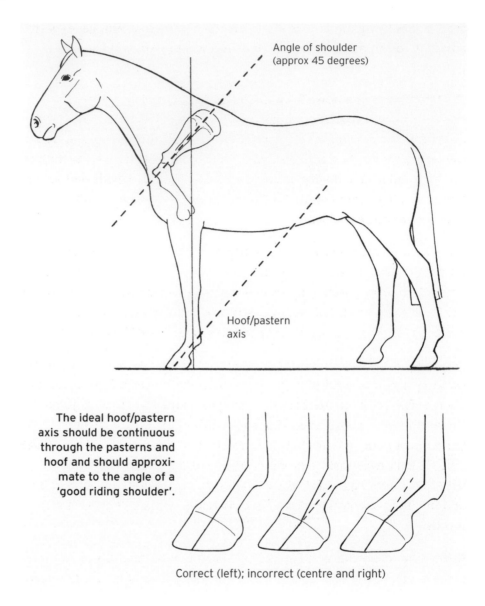

Angle of shoulder
(approx 45 degrees)

Hoof/pastern
axis

The ideal hoof/pastern axis should be continuous through the pasterns and hoof and should approximate to the angle of a 'good riding shoulder'.

Correct (left); incorrect (centre and right)

Limbs

Going up from the feet, you want to see a good, continuous hoof/pastern axis (HPA). In simple terms, it is accepted that the ideal angle of a 'good riding shoulder' from the point of the withers to the point of the shoulder is about 45 degrees and that an ideal HPA should be very close to that. A poor hoof/pastern axis (in which the angle is 'broken' either forwards or backwards in the region of the coronet) is caused sometimes by poor conformation and sometimes by poor farriery (common causes are the toes being too long or the heels too high) – so again, get expert advice if you think there is a problem and want to know if it can be put right.

When you look at a horse from the front, you should be able to draw two lines from the points of the shoulders to the ground that are parallel, bisect the forelegs and make angles of 90 degrees with the ground. From the side, a perpendicular line should bisect the foreleg, touch the bulb of the heel and form a 90-degree angle with the ground. Any deviations are faults, but, depending on their degree, not necessarily ones with the potential to cause problems.

If the measurement between the centre of the horse's hooves is greater than that between the points of his shoulders, he is base wide. This often occurs in narrow-chested horses and can put extra strain on the inside of the forelegs and feet. The opposite scenario is the horse who is base narrow, which can put extra strain and concussion on the outsides.

Relatively long forearms and short cannon bones make for limbs which stand up to stress. A lot of emphasis is often put on the amount of bone a horse has (the circumference of the widest part of the foreleg, just below the knee) as this affects his ability to carry weight. However, lightness of bone (a term that refers to external measurement, not actual quality) isn't necessarily a problem as long as the cannon bone isn't itself much too long – and whilst Arabs may sometimes look to be light of bone, the bone itself is denser and therefore stronger than in many breeds.

Knees should be wide and flat and you need to look carefully at how the cannon bone comes out of this very important joint. There are two main common faults: back at the knee and over at the knee.

The horse who is back at the knee has a concave outline between the bottom of the knee and the top of the fetlock. This conformation fault puts extra strain on the tendons and makes the horse more susceptible to concussive stress, so unless it is very mild, it is not something you would want to see – particularly in an eventer or showjumper. If the outline is convex, the horse is over at the knee; again, it puts extra stress on tendons and ligaments, but given a choice most horsemen regard it as the lesser of the two evils. As with all potential problems, everything is a matter of degree.

Pasterns should be reasonably long and sloping to absorb shocks, but if they are too long, the fetlock drops too low and puts extra strain on tendons and ligaments. Upright pasterns make for an uncomfortable ride and because they are inefficient at absorbing concussion, the horse will be more prone to associated problems such as ringbone and navicular. (Hind pasterns are naturally slightly shorter than front ones.)

Moving to the hind limbs, if you look at the horse from the side you should be able to drop an imaginary perpendicular line from the point of the buttock to the ground and see it touch the point of the hock before running down the back of the cannon bone. From behind, your line should pass through the centre of the hock, fetlock and foot.

It is often said that a horse's engine is behind the saddle – and the hock is one of the most important components. Sickle hocks, where the leg is in front of the perpendicular, are weak hocks. Cow hocks, where the hocks turn inwards, are not usually such a problem from the soundness point of view unless the defect is pronounced.

Body

For most disciplines, the ideal frame is one that is reasonably compact. However, a horse with a markedly short back is prone to problems that may be directly or indirectly related to his conformation: he is more likely to overreach and it will often be difficult to fit a saddle. In simple terms, if there isn't enough room for a saddle, then it may be inevitable that some of the rider's weight may impinge on the loins, which are not strong enough to bear it. This can lead to back problems and, with such conformation, you really do need an excellent saddle fitter who can make use of the latest advances in saddle-making to avoid causing discomfort or pain.

It used to be said that short-backed horses were good jumpers, but riders at top level have now moved away from that point of view. They say that to make the distances in combinations, horses need a reasonable length of body. However, in showjumping as well as all the other disciplines, an overlong back is inevitably weaker. Mares are naturally longer in the back than geldings and stallions, to allow room for carrying a foal; interestingly, a slightly long back is also held to be acceptable in Connemara ponies, as they were bred to carry panniers of seaweed behind a rider.

Both markedly dipped backs and their opposite, pronounced roach backs, are conformation faults that reduce the horse's biomechanical efficiency. Again, the risk depends on the extent of the problem and it is essential that your saddle suits the profile of the back (see Chapter 4). Whatever the conformation of the back, you need depth through the girth (as opposed to a 'shallow girth') to allow room for the heart and lungs. Even when a horse is lean, muscled and fully fit for racing or top-level eventing, depth of girth will be easy to see.

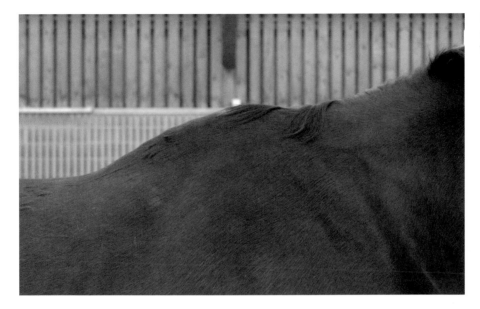

High withers can make it difficult to fit a saddle.

Head, neck and shoulders

Whilst most of us appreciate a nice head, whether it be the chiselled head of a blood horse or the workmanlike one of a cob this – unless it is so large and heavy that it affects the horse's balance – is the least important part of an animal's conformation. However, the way the head is set onto the neck and how the neck comes out from the withers have a big effect on the horse's way of going.

There should be enough space behind the jawbone for the horse to flex easily. From the side, you want to see a U-shape where the jaw runs into the throat, rather than a V-shape. The latter fault, often described as being 'thick through the jaw', means that the horse cannot flex easily because his windpipe will be bent and it will be more difficult for him to breathe. It might be that in some cases, it does not matter whether a horse flexes and goes in a more collected outline – but his natural way of going will then be with his nose ahead of the vertical, which will mean he is tighter through his back. Arabs naturally go with their heads and tails up, but they are usually clean through the jaw and can be as soft and swinging through their backs as any other horse.

Look at the angle at which the neck comes out from the withers, but at the same time, be aware of breed characteristics. Thoroughbreds and Quarter Horses are bred for speed and, as such, to have a lower head carriage, so their necks are often set on lower than, say, the modern Warmblood bred for dressage and jumping. There is nothing to prevent them succeeding in disciplines other than that for which they were originally bred – as, obviously, many do – but it is important to give them time to build up muscles and adapt to a way of going that may not come as easily to them as to other breeds and types.

The only type of neck conformation that really can be a weak link is the true ewe neck. Don't confuse the horse who is lacking in muscle with the horse who is truly (skeletally) ewe-necked. The first will improve with correct feeding and work, but you won't be able to change the second –

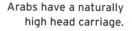

Arabs have a naturally high head carriage.

you will have to settle for working within the animal's limitations and will often find he is stiff through his back.

For a riding animal, you need shoulders with enough slope to give a comfortable ride. Draught breeds have – and need – straighter shoulders to give them 'pulling power', but this conformation usually goes with upright pasterns and makes for a horse who is not so comfortable under saddle and is more prone to concussion problems. As always, it's a case of horses for courses – but if you are trying to get a straight-shouldered animal fit for medium to high level endurance riding, you may find he is more susceptible to problems such as ringbone.

The straighter shoulders of heavy horses give them pulling power.

Temperament

Some people might think that temperament has nothing to do with getting a horse fit, but it can have a big effect on everything from feeding to the work you do. For instance, whilst you can't turn a Dobbin into a racehorse by feeding the equivalent of rocket fuel in a bag, or turn a hyperactive, highly bred animal into a happy hack through calming supplements, you can use the latest nutritional research to minimize problems (see Chapter 3).

Although there are exceptions, cold-blooded horses with a lot of heavy or draught horse influence are often more naturally laid back than those with a high percentage of Thoroughbred or Arab blood. The former – not just because of their temperaments, but because of their metabolism and structure – often take longer to get fit, though it can be done. On the other hand, the 'blood horse' who always comes out raring to go may be easier to get reasonably fit, but you will need to monitor him carefully to make sure he is building enough stamina, especially when you are hoping to reach a fitness peak for serious competition. There have been many cases of horses in top-level horse trials who have 'run out of petrol' on the last stages of the cross-country course because they appeared to be full of running at the start but were lacking that final edge to their fitness.

Health and condition

A heavy worm burden is debilitating and dangerous.

Before you can start to think about tailoring a fitness programme, you need to make sure that your horse is in good health and assess his condition. If he has a problem such as teeth that need rasping or a worm burden, it is going to affect his well-being and his work. In the long term, you could find yourself with a horse going nowhere.

It might sound like an exaggeration, but if you think it through, it makes sense to pay attention to detail right from the start. For instance, step one on the road to disappointment is a horse with sharp edges on his teeth or discomfort caused by wolf teeth interfering with the bit. Step two is a horse who carries himself badly and probably fights the rider, setting up stresses and strains in other parts of his body –

notably the neck and back. Step three is a horse who is more prone to injury because of the above.

It also makes sense to analyse his current condition before you start a fittening programme and perhaps altering his diet to go with it. If he is too fat, he will need a weight reduction plan and plenty of slow work to avoid the risk of putting too much strain, too soon, on his heart and lungs. If he is too thin, he will need a feed plan that enables you to supply energy and the basics for building muscle. And whilst it is always important to pay careful attention to the fit of your tack, the overweight or underweight horse in 'soft' condition is more prone to rubs and galls, which apart from being a sign of poor horse management will mean time off work whilst they heal.

Signs of a healthy horse

Whilst it is relatively easy to list the statistics that go to indicate a healthy horse – temperature, respiration, pulse rate, etc. – working out how your horse feels means knowing him as an individual. This means that you know his usual demeanour and can spot when something might be wrong. For instance, if he is usually the sort who has his head over the door to see everything that is going on in the yard, or comes to the gate the moment someone appears, warning bells will ring if he is lethargic or uninterested. But if he enjoys his beauty sleep and it's quite normal for him to do no more than twitch an ear when you disturb it, you probably don't need to make a panic call to the vet every time you find him dozing.

Does your horse have his normal alert look when you go to see him?

Vets often talk about the ABC of horse observation: Appearance, Behaviour and Condition. This means being aware of how your horse looks and behaves through your daily routine so you know when something is not quite right. Most people should recognize when a horse is lame or suffering from colic, but not everyone is as good at spotting the early warning signs. As a guideline, here are some ideas to help you assess your horse through the normal interaction you enjoy each day through looking after and riding him: I've assumed that he is stabled overnight, but if he lives out, you will be able to adapt them easily enough:

? Does he greet you in his usual way, whether it is with ears pricked and a whinny, an impatient banging of the door with a forefoot, or a grumpy face that means you can never be early enough with his breakfast?

? Give him a quick visual and manual once-over. Are there any obvious signs of injury: blood, swelling, heat in the limbs? It's amazing how many people arrive at their horse's box still half asleep and have fed or even mucked out before they notice that he is bleeding or resting a swollen leg. Is his demeanour in the box as you would expect it, or does he seem depressed or unusually grumpy? Is he moving normally round the box or, when you ask him to move over, does he seem stiff or reluctant? Is his respiration normal or does his breathing seem fast or laboured?

? Has he eaten all his feed and hay? If he is normally an enthusiastic eater and there is some left – particularly hard feed – it can be a danger sign.

? Has he drunk the usual amount of water? This may vary according to moisture levels in haylage or soaked hay and grass consumption, but a dehydrated horse is a horse in trouble. If you pinch the skin on his neck, it should spring back immediately you release it; if the skin takes time to go down, it is almost certainly a sign of dehydration.

? Is his bedding as you normally find it? This could range from a mixed up mess of bedding and droppings to – if you are a really lucky owner – a neat and tidy pile of droppings in one corner. If the bedding is noticeably scraped up in one corner or side of the box, check for scrapes on the walls or door that suggest your horse might have got cast. If he seems subdued, has he had or is he harbouring colic?

? Are his droppings usual in number and consistency? Fewer piles, particularly if the droppings are harder than usual, can be a warning of current or incipient colic caused basically because the horse is constipated. Pronounced diarrhoea can be anything from a sudden change in diet – perhaps a sudden flush of grass – to stress. Is the bedding markedly wetter or drier than usual?

? When you take off his rug, do you find that he been sweating? If so, does he show other signs of discomfort or has he simply been too hot – which obviously means you have over-rugged him?

? Does his coat lie flat, or is it staring? Common sense applies here, because an animal with a thick winter coat will not have the sleek, flat coat of a rugged-up Thoroughbred in winter. The hairs in an unclipped, unrugged horse's coat will stand on end to trap a layer of air, which is nature's way of keeping him warm. If he seems bright-eyed and bushy-tailed in all other ways, you are unlikely to have a problem, but if he shows other signs such as lethargy or nasal discharge, check him out thoroughly.

? Is there any discharge from his nostrils or eyes?

? When you run your hand over each part of his body, perhaps as part of your grooming routine, and down each leg in turn, are there any signs of heat or swelling? Are there any signs of soreness in the saddle area? When you pick up and clean out his feet, are his shoes secure and in good condition and is there anything trapped in a foot? Don't assume that because you picked his feet out the night before, they are bound to be fine in the morning: I once found I had a lame horse with a large splinter wedged into the frog. It was a 'foreign body' that I hadn't spotted in a bale of top brand shavings – even though it had been sifted carefully.

? When you lead him out, does he move normally or are there unusual signs of stiffness? If so, trot him up to see if he is lame.

TPR

Although observation will alert you to possible problems, it's important to know and check regularly your horse's temperature, pulse and respiration, usually referred to as TPR.

Temperature: On many competition yards, horses' temperatures are taken daily so that an average can be worked out. Vets and researchers advise that every owner should do this, as a rise in temperature is usually the first sign of illness. Temperature should be taken at the same time each day. The average 'normal' reading for an adult horse is 37–38 °C, or 100–101 °F; as you would expect, it is normal for the temperature to be slightly higher after exercise.

A temperature of more than 40 °F or 102.5 °F is potentially serious and means you should ask your vet's advice. A very low temperature is also a danger sign.

Using a stethoscope to check a horse's heart rate.

Pulse: The easiest way to take a horse's pulse, or heart rate, is via the facial artery under the jaw. You can either count for a full minute or use the easier and generally recommended method of counting the number of beats in 15 seconds and multiplying by four. It is also possible to feel and count the heartbeat on the left-hand side of the chest, just behind the elbow where the girth sits. A normal pulse rate is 35–42 beats per minute for a horse at rest and it will be faster after exercise or if the horse is in pain or excited. When you're sitting on a horse, you can sometimes actually feel the heart rate increase if he sees something that worries or excites him.

Respiration: The usual way to count the respiration rate is to stand behind and to one side of the horse and count the breaths: each rise and fall of his flanks, with a slight pause in between, counts as one breath. The normal respiratory rate at rest is between 8 and 20 breaths per minute.

Condition scoring

As one person's idea of good or bad condition is not necessarily another's – for instance, in the show ring, where what some riders refer to as 'well covered' many others label 'fat' – the best way to assess a horse is to use the accepted method of condition scoring, as explained below. However, you need to apply this with common sense: for instance, a Thoroughbred will inevitably look leaner than a cob even when both are at the same stage of fitness, and a three-day event horse fit to run at Badminton may share some characteristics of the horse in poor condition – in particular, a prominent croup – but actually be at the peak of athleticism, with well-defined muscles but no excess fat.

Coats can hide a multitude of sins, too. You may just be able to see the ribs of a thin-skinned animal with a fine coat, such as a Thoroughbred, from some angles, but that does not necessarily mean that he is too thin. On the other hand, gently pushing your fingers into the thick coat of a pony may show that underneath all the hair is a ribby frame in need of extra food.

Condition scoring can be expressed in terms of 0–5 and different levels may be acceptable for different jobs. For instance, a top-level eventer or endurance horse may look to be in moderate condition when he is actually supremely fit: you need to take into account other factors such as how long it takes him to recover after exercise and his overall demeanour. A show horse should ideally be in good condition, but unfortunately too many are still fat and even obese. The basic criteria for condition scoring are as follows:

0 – Very poor. The rump is very sunken and there is a deep cavity under the tail. The skin looks as if it is tight over the skeleton and the backbone, ribs and pelvis are all prominent. The horse will look as if he has a ewe neck ('upside down') even when this is not actually the case.

1 – Poor. All the above apply, but to a slightly lesser extent.

2 – Moderate. The ribs are just visible, the neck is firm but narrow and the rump is flat either side of the spine, though the spine itself is not visible. Ribs can usually be seen, though not markedly so as with the first two categories.

3 – Good. The ribs can be felt but are covered, the rump is rounded and the neck is firm without being cresty.

4 – Fat. There is a gutter along the back and rump and it is difficult to feel the ribs and pelvis.

5 – Obese. The gutter along the back and rump is deep, the ribs cannot be felt and there are pads of fat – usually on the crest, body and shoulders.

Work rate

The last part of the equation needed to complete a picture of your horse is his current workload, as this will affect the work you give him from now on and how you feed him. Nutritionists say that most owners over-estimate their horses' workloads and that far fewer horses are actually in hard work than their riders fondly imagine. On the other hand, don't make the mistake of thinking that dressage and showing are always the easy options: factor in the preparation work and the inevitable stress of travelling, etc. and your horse has to cope with more than you might assume. The following guidelines from Spillers Horse Feeds may make a few riders think again:

Maintenance – horses and ponies not in work.

Light work – hacking and leisure riding, 1–2 hours per day; showing at local level; Preliminary/Novice to Elementary level dressage; showjumping at local shows, BSJA British Novice and Discovery classes; endurance rides up to 32 km (20 miles) at a slow pace, including sponsored rides; unaffiliated novice one-day events.

Medium work – showing on the affiliated circuit; affiliated dressage at Elementary to Medium and Advanced Medium level; BSJA Newcomers and Foxhunters level; BE Intermediate and Advanced one-day events; 50-mile (80-km) endurance rides; fast canter work for racing.

Hard work – affiliated dressage at Grand Prix level; BE three and four star three-day events; endurance race rides; racehorses in full training and racing.

Case history

Rehabilitating to fitness

At first glance, including the work of the International League for the Protection of Horses (ILPH) in a book about getting horses fit might seem unusual. But when you look at the work of its four centres and the lessons we can all learn from them, you get a perfect picture of what it means to take a holistic approach to getting horses fit for particular jobs. In some cases, those jobs may be limited, but in others, for example that of ILPH Penny, the animals exceed all expectations. ILPH Penny was taken into Penny Farm, its Blackpool recovery and rehabilitation centre, with a list of problems including ringworm, mange and a bad temper. Nine months later, she was spotted as having potential for the King's Troop as a gun horse and was one of those used at the Queen Mother's funeral.

Rehabilitating horses the ILPH way involves true teamwork, involving staff at the centres and outside specialists. Tony Tyler, its director of operations, defines rehabilitation as 'to restore to a former state of health' – but points out that, in some cases, animals achieved a better state of health than they had ever enjoyed before. The ILPH is not a sanctuary and, where possible, rehabilitated animals are rehomed on loan to suitable borrowers; they always remain the property of the charity and are inspected regularly by its team of field officers, in most cases former members of mounted police units.

Animals come to the centres in a variety of ways: many are welfare cases, others come through the ILPH's legacy and wills scheme – where it is hoped owners will, in leaving their animals, include a financial contribution to help cover the cost of assessing and hopefully rehoming them – and others may be taken in after individual rehabilitation requests. However, it is not an easy way out for owners who lose interest or do not want to take the final responsibility of having a horse who no longer has sufficient quality of life put down.

Horses, ponies and the occasional donkey arrive with a variety of problems. Disease problems are relatively scarce – though all are isolated and undergo investigations by a vet, farrier and perhaps, when applicable, a specialist such as a McTimoney practitioner working with veterinary permission. However, poor nutrition, ranging from slight to actual starvation, is a common problem.

The ILPH is also seeing an increasing number of foot problems, ranging from appallingly overgrown feet resembling Turkish slippers to animals who have been subjected to radical trimming that had caused actual suffering. Lameness and problems affecting backs, teeth and skin are seen frequently and conformation problems are also a factor. As Tony Tyler points out, you can't do much about conformation problems, but you can make sensible decisions about the jobs the animals can do in the future. The ILPH's farm managers say that many conformation problems are down to poor breeding, and not just at the bottom end of the scale: horses have come to the ILPH because, for instance, there is a demand in some quarters for 18 hh dressage horses. Huge horses do not always stand up to athletic demands and whilst some people can maintain and train them correctly, others are not so skilled.

With every animal who comes into the ILPH, there are common questions that are always asked:

- What is the aim and what can realistically be achieved from the animal?

- How long will it take? (As Tony Tyler puts it, rehabilitation is 'as long as a piece of string'.)

- What will it cost? The charity is often questioned on the amount of money spent on rehabilitating individual horses and people are often surprised at the average of £4,000 – but if you look at the cost of putting a horse into full livery and factor in everything from feed to veterinary bills, that sum can suddenly seem a surprisingly small amount.

- Will rehabilitation be fair to the horse? For example, a pony was dropped off at the gates of Hall Farm after she had been bitten by an Alsatian. The wounds had gone into the joint capsule and though everything that could be done to give her a fighting chance was done, the decision had to be made eventually that it was in the pony's best interest for her to be humanely destroyed.

Rehabilitation in practice

Michele Thornton is the manager of ILPH Hall Farm, having joined the organization in 2003. She previously trained and spent fifteen years at the renowned Porlock Vale equestrian centre and graduated from working pupil to chief instructor and stable manager. She has worked in National Hunt and point-to-point yards, spent some time as director of riding at Millfield School and has competed up to Prix St Georges level in dressage and Intermediate level in eventing; she has also trained two of her own horses to Grand Prix level dressage. Michele, who clearly has great personal experience in preparing horses for a variety of disciplines, makes the point that the ILPH is not not in the business of fittening horses for a particular discipline – it is trying to get them 'fit for life'.

Michele Thornton, manager of ILPH Hall Farm, Norfolk.

MICHELE THORNTON

The whole horse approach

Horses who come here may be broken physically, mentally or both. We're making them fit for a job in life. They arrive for a variety of reasons, ranging from laminitis to behavioural problems; behavioural problems are, almost without exception, related to things such as saddle fitting or foot pain caused through inappropriate shoeing: when a horse hurts in one area, it will cause problems in another. For instance, a laminitic animal may develop bone spavin or back spasm because of the way he holds himself to try and minimize the pain in his feet.

When a horse arrives, for whatever reason, he is put in isolation for a minimum of two weeks.

Because of the nature of the horses we take in, our vet, Andy Williamson, and our farrier, John Blake, are involved within 24 hours of his arrival. They work together and will observe the horse standing and in walk and trot. During the time that the horse is in isolation we do regular checks: temperature, pulse and respiration, condition scoring, de-worming and de-lousing. Daily notes are written on each horse so that we can refer back – that way, you know you have an accurate record of a horse's reactions, way of going and behaviour and are not relying on your memory.

When it's appropriate, we give the horse a substantial period of time at grass, which gives him time to 'be a horse' and hopefully heal some of the traumas he has been through. Spending time foraging, with his head down, stretching, is the best exercise you can give a horse: it doesn't matter what time of year it is, turnout is an essential part of getting him fit for life. Obviously we're very lucky in that we have good grazing of different types, with shelter.

We spend quite a lot of time getting a horse into an appropriate herd group. Some are sub-servient, others dominant; youngsters tend to run together and we tend to put animals of similar sizes together. However, if we have a pony who will eventually perhaps go from here to become a companion to a horse, we get him used to being with a bigger field companion.

Other horses impose discipline when needed. If we have one who is a bully, we have a wonder-ful mule who will put him straight without hurting him. If a horse is timid, he will go into what we call a 'smiley' group. The variety of paddocks we have is very useful; some paddocks are absolutely flat, whilst others are on a slope, so we can encourage the sort of movement patterns that benefit particular horses.

Horses are given as much time as they need out in the field; it will always be at least six weeks but if a horse needs eighteen months, that's fine. They are brought in every four to six weeks to see the farrier and may also be given treatment by our reg-ular McTimoney practitioner, Peggy Softey, or char-tered physiotherapists, Jo Speers and Kate Hulse, and will come in to see the dentist as needed. We're observing them all the time, noting things such as their coat conditions. Good old-fashioned stock-manship is very important – an eye for a horse, a feel for a horse – but I always try to have an open mind. I believe it's important to listen to everyone, from the newest members of staff to the 'old boys' who have been round horses all their lives.

Getting to work

Once we decide that a horse is sound, well and happy – and the horse's state of mind is as important as his physical well-being in terms of rehabilitation – we will look at starting a work programme. All horses go through a breaking programme from scratch, even if they have already been ridden, to highlight any possible problem areas. For instance, if a horse is insecure about being mounted, or is reluctant to lunge on one rein, we know that we have to restore his confidence or that perhaps he is showing signs of pain or discomfort. We like horses to go from here being safe to lunge on both reins and we use lungeing for different purposes – there is lungeing for exercise, lungeing for rehabilitation and lungeing for schooling purposes.

We do a lot of lungeing, leading and long-reining, depending on the horse's needs. When you work a horse on the ground you can see an awful lot – for instance, he might not use one hind leg as well as the other when he turns one way. There are also a lot of horses who could not start ridden work straight away because they have too much muscle wastage to take the weight of a rider. We always start in walk and I want to see a horse doing what I like to describe as a 'power walk' with his back swinging and his head and neck down. If you work a horse productively in walk for 20 minutes you can achieve a raised heart rate and get him sweating, if that is what you're trying to achieve, and you can encourage him both to go straight and to bend on each rein.

Pole work plays a huge role in our regime and my assistant manager, Sue Hodgkins, is particu-larly skilled at this. Just walking a serpentine around poles on the ground will highlight stiff-ness on one side and show you how a horse uses his limbs – we call it the slalom. We also do pole work in straight lines, usually using four poles in a row at appropriate distances; if we want to encourage the horse to lift his abdominal muscles, the distances will be shorter and to free the shoulder, they will be longer.

We don't use any side reins or other training aids, because we want to see how the horse carries himself naturally; we lunge from a cavesson, but tend to put a bridle on as well because a bridle means work. Working the horse 'naked' means you can see whether the muscles are rippling, and

Hall Farm's deputy manager, Sue Hodgkins, demonstrates the slalom exercise.

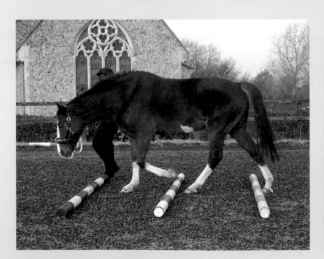

Pole work can encourage the horse to free his shoulders and lift his abdominal muscles.

Different combinations of poles can be used to improve the horse's co-ordination.

not having a roller or saddle on – unless there is a particular reason for doing so – means there is no chance of the muscles being blocked. We are reading what the horse is telling us: the shape he wants to take; why he wants to go with his head twisted to one side. The quality of work you can get from a sound horse without extra tack is phenomenal.

Also, you don't need extra equipment to encourage the horse to stretch and build up the muscles he needs to carry a rider – by pointing the whip down towards the back of the hindquarters you encourage the back end to work, whilst vibrating the lunge rein gently encourages the horse to lower his head. Having said that, we do lunge from the bridle sometimes: we have a 17.2 hh giant who would say 'thanks very much' and be off if you lunged him from a cavesson.

We do quite a lot of long-reining before riding to get the horse to stop, start and turn and we're lucky in that we can long-rein for miles without going on the roads. At the same time, we can show horses so many of the things they are going to meet in the big world; we get enough traffic on our drive to assess their reactions and can go parallel to the A11 and introduce them to the idea of fast, heavy traffic in a safe environment. Long-reining in a straight line helps enormously; you can see whether the hips are swinging and whether the horse is pushing with both hind limbs, and you can ask for a bit of bend by stepping slightly to the left or right.

When we start to ride the horses, we are very traditional. We tend to mount from a mounting block as if you use a leg up, you need people who are good at both giving and receiving it! Also,

from the point of view of the horse's back and the saddle it's always best to mount from a block – even a 12.2 hh pony will be trained to stand to the mounting block. We don't have many problems backing horses because we've done so much preliminary work.

Michele schooling an ILPH horse who has been rehabilitated after admittance with physical problems.

Ridden work and groundwork are used in parallel so the horse still has a 'comfort zone.' Once the horse is safe and can stop, start, walk, trot and canter in the safe environment of the school, we will go out onto our walkways round the farm and when he feels happy and confident there, he will start schooling along traditional lines and be introduced to hacking. We do a lot of schooling out hacking, using different fields and encouraging them to work round and deep to an appropriate level to get their abdominals up. Anything you can do in the school you can do out hacking on the tracks: leg-yielding, cantering fifteen strides on the left lead then fifteen on the right, asking for shoulder-in and for lengthened strides. If you have slopes, you can ask for a little collection going down the hill and lengthened strides going up it; if a horse can canter up and canter down our field with the greatest slope, he's pretty balanced! Wherever you are, you can make use of the environment around you.

There is no magic in what we do. The only magical factor is time – time to recover, time in the field, time spent working in walk, time spent building up a work programme correctly.

Feeding

We feed purely what the horse needs. They are meant to eat grass and we have a variety of fields, including 'special needs' paddocks that are heavily grazed – and also heavily swept. This means that horses whose actual grass intake has to be limited can be turned out and have to work harder for the feed.

Horses who are not getting the calories they need from the grass will be fed hay or haylage on a needs basis. It's made from predominantly cocksfoot and Timothy grasses and is very high in fibre and very tasty. Grazing will be supplemented as needed: if we have an incredibly mild autumn they might not need extra forage until January, but if there is a lot of rain and colder weather we might be feeding it in October.

Wherever possible, horses live out 24/7. Reasons why this might not be possible include animals with photosensitization problems, those who are in isolation or under veterinary care and soundness issues. The only feeds we have are Dodson and Horrell Build-Up Mix, alfalfa chaff and sugar beet. We use a mix because usually, we're only feeding them to administer medication and this is the easiest way; alfalfa chaff is high in

calcium and good for youngsters and older horses and sugar beet is high in fibre. We feed garlic to horses with severe sweet itch but don't use any other supplements unless our vet or farrier suggests it.

Most people feed too much. A lot of owners get very confused about the difference between light, medium and hard work – hard work is going round the Grand National course! To me, light work is what most of us do in an average week: hacking two or three times, schooling two or three times and the occasional sponsored ride or competition. We all hugely underestimate the feed value of grass, which is something that can cause obvious problems such as laminitis and can be a contributory factor to some behavioural problems.

Tack and equipment

I take a very simple approach to bitting. Just about the only bits we have in our tack room are eggbutt snaffles, double bridles – which are used more for staff training purposes than for anything else – and Chifneys if needed for control when leading, but only in exceptional circumstances as even these can cause more problems than they solve. I was trained in a purist way and have kept that philosophy; I feel that if a horse can't be ridden in a simple eggbutt there is usually a problem with his teeth, his back or his rider!

We have a variety of saddles in different widths and qualified saddle fitters are important members of the ILPH teams. Because a lot of the horses who come here have muscle wastage – which may or may not have been caused, at least in part, by badly fitting saddles – we fit wider than many people perhaps would, to allow for muscles to build up.

2 Systems analysis

WHEN YOU AIM TO get a horse fit, it is tempting to think of the state of fitness as one package – and the 'big picture' is, of course, important. However, it can also be helpful to look at all the systems within your horse's body that need to be worked on, as forgetting a key component can lead to problems.

Researchers now talk about the need for a four-pronged approach to fitness in horses and humans, looking at the cardiovascular, respiratory, skeletal and muscular systems. It sounds complicated, but in fact knowledgeable riders have been doing it for years without putting labels on it. Hunting yards and those bringing horses back into work after a break have always been told to do six weeks of slow work to 'harden the legs', starting with two to three weeks of walk exercise before bringing in short periods of trot and eventually canter.

By doing this, you subject the horse's body to stress – because any effort imposes stress – but not so much that it causes a problem. As work gradually increases, so does the body's ability to adapt and to cope with it. Cardiovascular and respiratory fitness mean that the horse's pulse and breathing rates returns to their normal resting rates within an acceptable time whilst skeletal fitness, in basic terms, enables the horse to work without going lame. Muscular fitness means that the horse's muscles take up oxygen effectively and get rid of metabolic waste efficiently.

The heart of the matter

The cardiovascular system – the heart and all the vessels through which it pumps blood – performs a number of functions, the most fundamental of which are that it takes oxygen and nutrients to the body tissue and also takes harmful substances such as lactic acid away. It also plays an important role in thermoregulation, carrying heat around the body.

The heart of an adult horse weighs on average about 4 kg (8.8 lb) and in athletic terms, a large heart is preferable to a smaller one as it pumps a greater volume of blood with every beat. As a horse becomes fit, the actual size of his heart increases; some researchers say the amount can be as much as one-third.

We all know that when we make a greater physical effort, such as running, our heart rate increases and the same applies to a horse. This is the body's way of getting oxygen to the muscles more quickly. But as a horse becomes fitter, the stroke volume of the heart also increases: this means that it is able to pump a larger amount of blood through at each beat.

As detailed in Chapter 1, the average heart rate for a horse at rest is around 35–42 beats per minute; the rates for young or unfit horses are usually at the higher end of the scale and rates for older or fit ones are at the lower end. In a really fit horse, you may find a resting heart rate as low as 26–27 beats per minute – and when he is working at full peak, it may rise to around 240.

In terms of athleticism, the best combination is a large heart with a low resting heartbeat. An elevated heart rate that is not a result of exertion is often a sign of pain (which is why horses suffering from colic will often exhibit this), excitement or fear. This shows why it is important to know your horse's average resting heart rate during all phases of getting him fit. As a general rule, his heart rate should return to the normal base rate within 10 minutes of whatever work he has done being completed – and if it doesn't, he has been worked too hard for his current state of fitness.

Fortunately, heart abnormalities are much rarer in horses than in humans. The most common is arrythmia, an irregular rhythm picked up when a horse is at rest. This rarely causes problems, because the correct beat is restored when the horse becomes active. Actual 'heart attacks' are, fortunately, rare in horses, which is why they receive wide reporting when they happen to, for instance, well-known racehorses. Aneurisms, which push out and weaken artery walls, are infrequent but more common than heart attacks. They are usually linked to a build-up of worm larvae, which underlines the necessity of a proper worming programme.

Thermoregulation

The body has a temperature band within which it works efficiently. If its temperature goes above or below that, its efficiency is compromised, so a number of mechanisms exist which act to keep the body's temperature within the correct band – a process known as thermoregulation. Because of the work we ask horses to do, it is more likely that they risk becoming too hot, rather than too cold. A certain amount of heat is necessary for muscles, tendons and ligaments to work efficiently, hence the term 'warming up', but the level of heating has to be controlled and the main mechanism for this is the production and evaporation of sweat.

If the process of thermoregulation is compromised, the horse can become ill, or even die. In fact, there have been cases of endurance horses competing in extreme conditions actually dying, which is why the sport has come under rigorous scrutiny and veterinary regulation has become so important.

It is therefore important both to warm up a horse before asking for concerted effort and also to ensure that he cools down – or can be cooled down using external methods – when he becomes too hot, especially in hot, humid conditions.

The efficiency of a horse's thermoregulation is affected by a number of factors, including his size, the thickness of his coat and weather conditions: temperature, humidity and wind speed. The speed at which a horse can lose heat depends mainly on the ratio of his surface area to his bodyweight. As this ratio usually becomes smaller as the body size increases, small horses are more efficient at cooling down but not so good at retaining body heat when the temperature drops. This is why, after the research into the effects of combined heat and humidity on horses, led by a team at the UK's Animal Health Trust before the Olympic Games in Atlanta (1996), the physical blueprint for the ideal event horse emerged as a 16 hh Thoroughbred rather than a 16.3 hh Warmblood or heavier horse. Horse sports, along with everything else, have become affected by global warming: combined heat and humidity has become more common throughout the UK and Europe, not just in parts of the world where it has long been the norm (see Chapter 6).

Muscle power

There are three types of muscle: skeletal, cardiac and smooth. Skeletal muscles, as the name suggests, move bones by contracting and stretching in opposing pairs. They are attached to the bones by tendons, which have a small amount of elasticity.

Muscles have fibres which work in different ways and are now labelled as type I, type IIA and type IIB. The predominance of particular types has a big influence on whether a horse is naturally designed for speed and power or for endurance. Horses who compete successfully in disciplines where speed and/or power are important, such as sprinters on the Flat, showjumpers and polo ponies, usually have more type IIB fibres, whilst endurance stars have a predominance of type I and IIA fibres.

The function of the muscles is linked to oxygen, delivered through the blood, and glycogen. They store both oxygen and glycogen; glycogen comes from glucose which is not immediately needed and is therefore stored in the muscle fibres. If demand for oxygen exceeds supply, lactic acid forms in the cells and can lead to the painful and debilitating condition commonly known as azoturia but nowadays labelled as exertional rhabdomyolysis. Proper fittening will not only improve a horse's ability to take up and deliver oxygen to the muscles, it will also enable him to eliminate waste products more efficiently.

Muscle damage can have many causes, ranging from azoturia to dehydration as well as overexertion and even a poorly fitting saddle.

Whilst skeletal muscle needs stimulation from the nervous system to work, cardiac (heart) muscle contracts on its own (involuntarily). Unlike skeletal muscle, it does not get tired but the speed of its contractions can obviously change according to how hard the body is working. It will also speed up under stress, such as when a horse is nervous, excited or in pain. The smooth or viscous muscle found in the walls of organs such as the bladder and digestive tract also works involuntarily.

Boning up

The horse's skeleton is much more than something which keeps the insides in and the outside, out! As well as providing a framework for the body and protection for vital organs, it enables the horse to move. Also, blood cells and platelets – the latter essential to ensure that blood will clot after an injury – are made in bone marrow.

Bone itself is a mixture of protein tissue and minerals. So although we may think of bones as 'dead' inflexible structures that don't change, they not only have slight flexibility but can remodel in response to stress. This is important in terms of fitness, because healthy remodelling is essential for soundness and strength. It also underlines why it is important for horses to have plenty of time in the field, so they are moving around.

The horse's skeleton comprises more than 200 bones, supported by ligaments – fibrous tissue which in basic terms keeps everything together and supports the overall structure. The joints between bones range from those which allow a great range of movement, such as in the hock, through ones with a slight amount, as between the vertebrae, to fused joints, as in the skull.

Joints can move in a variety of ways. Some are hinged, as at the fetlock; some, as in the hip, work on a ball and socket basis. Others, such as those between the skull and first two cervical vertebrae, pivot. In some joints, such as the knee and hock, the bones 'slide' over each other. Joints with the greatest range of movement consist of bones with ends coated with cartilage, which has an essential role in withstanding concussion. The joint is lubricated by synovial fluid (joint fluid) which acts like oil in an engine and helps keep the parts moving smoothly. Even fixed or limited range joints also have cartilage and/or connective tissue between the bones. The horse has a unique locking arrangement in all four legs called the stay mechanism which allows him to sleep standing up.

The horse's skeleton develops as he grows and bones grow through the activity of growth plates, found at the ends of the long bones in the limbs. These are made of cartilage, which gradually calcifies and becomes new bone – so the bones grow longer and the horse grows taller.

Growth plates close, or stop growing, at different ages according to their sites in the body. Standard veterinary opinion has been that this ranges from six to nine months up to two or two and a half years, but some researchers now believe that the process continues for up to five years – even longer in the case of large and slow-maturing breeds, such as the Irish Draught.

The cartilage covering the ends of bones also helps the joints to move smoothly. Young horses have a much higher percentage of cartilage than older ones; natural wear and tear through ageing reduces the amount of cartilage, which is why older horses – and their riders – are more prone to stiffness and osteoarthritis. Again, this has implications in getting a horse fit, both in terms of nutrition (see Chapter 3) and in the importance of warming up and cooling down.

Research has also found links between healthy bone growth and exercise. The latest research shows that Thoroughbred Flat racehorses given some training as 2-year-olds generally have longer careers than those whose training begins later. A study in New Zealand has also shown that early structured exercise in foals could be beneficial; in a group of thirty-six foals, half underwent 1,700 m (1,860 yards) of galloping in addition to their natural exercise at pasture, from the ages of 10 days onwards. When some of the horses were evaluated at the age of 18 months, there was no increase in either clinical disease or mechanical properties, but there was a significant and beneficial increase in living cartilage cells.

Orthopaedic surgeon Ian Wright says that research has shown that non-Thoroughbreds, in particular, Warmbloods, benefit from non-forced exercise to give some protection from osteochondrosis (OCD). In real terms, this means keeping them out as much as possible rather than stabling them for long periods.

Achieving 'skeletal fitness' is, in some respects, more difficult than fittening other systems in the body, because the changes made in response to gradually increased stress occur so slowly. It has been estimated that it takes about sixty days of riding five days a week for the density of the cannon bones to adapt to more strenuous activity – so whilst a horse might feel as if he is reasonably fit, some riders may simply not be riding often enough to have an effect on skeletal fitness.

A breath of fresh air

No horse can work well or achieve even a reasonable level of fitness if his respiratory system does not function well. Unfortunately, standard management means that the odds are stacked against him; stabling horses exposes their respiratory systems to constant threat from dust, mould spores and ammonia from urine and faeces. There are ways to minimize these threats, as discussed later in this chapter, but it is still thought that recurrent airway obstruction (RAO) affects up to 80 per cent of horses and ponies in many parts of the world, including the UK and northern Europe.

In some ways, the horse's respiratory system is badly designed. Whereas humans normally breathe through the nose but also breathe through the mouth during intensive exercise – and thus get more oxygen to the lungs, more quickly – horses can only breathe through their nostrils. This is one reason why some suffer from exercise induced pulmonary haemorrhage (EIPH.) Although it is fair to say that this is most often seen in racehorses, it can affect horses in all disciplines, including eventing.

As the horse breathes in, he takes air into the lungs, where a network of 'branches' end up as alveoli. It is in these that a process called gaseous exchange takes place: oxygen is taken into the red blood cells and transported round the body and carbon dioxide is expelled from the system. It is when the environmental threats mentioned above interfere with this process that the horse's health is threatened.

A natural facility called locomotor-respiratory coupling allows horses to breathe most effectively and economically in canter and gallop. Basically, breathing is linked to what scientists call locomotor forces, which include pressure of the organs in the abdomen on the diaphragm and the change in the body's axis caused by the rocking motion of these gaits. In simple terms, the horse breathes once for every stride he takes, as can be seen by analysis on a high-speed treadmill. This means that for disciplines in which the horse canters or gallops for long periods – in particular, racing and eventing – a horse with a longer stride is theoretically a more efficient athlete, as he can breathe more deeply.

Straight from the horse's mouth

So what do a horse's teeth and mouth have to do with fitness? More than you might think – as with so many aspects of getting a horse in good physical condition, the 'ripple effect' can have major implications. If a horse is unhappy in his mouth, either because he has wolf teeth that cause discomfort when the bit knocks against them or sharp edges on cheek teeth, he will resist the rider's aids. Depending on the severity of the problem and his temperament, this may range from mild resistance to a full-blown refusal to go in the way he is asked.

The more the rider insists, either through stronger rein aids or by tying down the horse's head – or both – the more the horse will stiffen and set his jaw. The knock-on effect is that he will stiffen through his neck, back and quarters, producing sore muscles. In the very worst scenario, this can lead to permanent damage: one highly respected chartered physiotherapist says that horses who have been forced into an outline with draw reins often have permanent damage to the nuchal ligament at the poll. That is not meant as an indictment of a particular training aid or of training aids in general, simply a warning that it is important to find out the reason for a schooling problem rather than aiming for a quick fix.

We also have to remember that we are often trying to educate young horses – and in the case of Flat racehorses, competing them at their peak – at a time when their teeth are constantly changing. Like babies, horses have two sets of teeth, deciduous or milk teeth and a permanent, adult set. Young horses start to lose their deciduous teeth from around $2\frac{1}{2}$ years onwards and will have a full adult set at about 5 years old.

Adult male horses usually have forty teeth and mares have thirty-six. All have six front, or incisor teeth, in each jaw; twelve cheek teeth, or premolars and twelve molars. Males also have four tushes, one at each side of the upper and lower jaw, which are what remains of canine teeth. Very occasionally, these are also found in mares, but are usually much smaller. Both sexes may develop shallow-rooted, vestigial premolars called wolf teeth, which can interfere with the action of the bit and are often removed as standard to prevent this happening.

If you look at any horse, you will see that his lower jaw is narrower than the upper one. This means that as he chews, the outside edges of the upper cheek teeth and the inside edges of the lower ones can be ground sharp, causing grazes or cuts to the cheeks and tongue. The upper and lower cheek teeth can also develop hooks, which interfere with the horse's ability to chew. If he can't chew properly, not only will he not get the full benefit from his food but the digestive process will be compromised and he may be more at risk of suffering colic. This is why it really does make sense to feed forage and hard feed from the ground, rather than in mangers and haynets or racks.

Feet first

As discussed in Chapter 1, feet with poor quality hoof horn or an incorrect hoof/pastern axis predispose a horse to problems whatever job he does. For instance, whilst vets and researchers know more than ever about navicular syndrome – and, just as important, that some cases previously thought to be navicular have been wrongly identified – this only goes to emphasize the importance of understanding why feet must be correctly balanced. For instance, if a horse's natural conformation or poor farriery results in low heels and this is coupled with long toes – perhaps because of too infrequent trimming – one of the consequences will be that too much pressure is exerted on the navicular bone by the deep digital flexor tendon.

When you look at what the hoof has to do, it is a miracle of living engineering. Not only does it support the horse's weight (at times, as when landing over a fence, all that weight momentarily on one foot) – it also has to limit concussion and prevent slipping.

Its structure is usually divided into two categories, the outer insensitive foot and the inner sensitive components. The outer foot comprises the wall (made up of dense horn), the sole and the frog; it houses the structures of the inner, sensitive foot, including bones, blood vessels and cartilage.

When we talk about poor quality feet, we usually focus on the outward signs: in particular, crumbling horn and/or hooves which don't grow enough to make up for the amount of normal wear. But in order for the horn to be in good enough condition to support the horse – and in most cases, for him to keep shoes on for four to six weeks at a time – it's important to take a 'whole horse' approach.

Horn is actually a specialized layer of skin which grows down from the coronary band. It is thickest at the toe, but more pliable at the heel. The periople, which looks like a layer of thick skin or membrane where the hoof meets the coronary band, acts as a protective film to control evaporation. Healthy horn grows continually at a rate of about 6–10 mm ($\frac{1}{4}$–$\frac{3}{8}$ in) per month. This means that new horn at the coronet will take, on average, about nine months to reach the ground.

The sole is the ground surface of the foot. It should be firm and thick and noticeably concave, especially in the hind feet. Horses with flat, thin soles are more prone to bruising.

The frog's main purpose is to allow enough expansion of the heels when weight bearing and to minimize the effects of concussion. It used to be thought that it also acts as a pump to aid circulation, but modern researchers say this is unproven.

When the horse stands square, his weight is naturally distributed so that about 60 per cent is taken by the forelegs and 40 per cent by the hind legs. This means that the forefeet are theoretically under more stress than the hind ones and certainly the hind feet are less susceptible to bruising, concussion and compressive forces.

So why do some horses have enviably hard, healthy feet whilst others can't keep shoes on for more than days at a time? One answer is genetics: sometimes you can have two horses with identical lifestyles, diets and workloads and one will have good feet whilst the other is a farrier's nightmare.

Some breeds are renowned for their tough feet. Fell ponies, for instance, have hard 'blue' horn that often allows them to work unshod. Others, such as the Thoroughbred, are notoriously prone to problems. But though there are a worrying number of Thoroughbreds with flat soles and poor horn quality, it isn't the horses' fault: it's ours. By breeding for specific characteristics – in this case, speed – at the expense of the basic building blocks of soundness, we have bred in problems.

The right lifestyle, bedding and day-to-day management all have an impact on hoof health as well as the overall well-being of your horse. For instance, all horses need regular exercise and exercise encourages hoof growth by increasing circulation. Standing in a stable for long periods means there is a constant load on the horse's feet and it also inhibits circulation. So, for the sake of his feet, as well as for the rest of his physical and mental well-being, keep him out as much as possible and make sure he has regular exercise.

If you're in a Catch 22 situation because crumbling hooves mean you can't give him sufficient work, ask your farrier and/or vet's advice about turning out your horse unshod on suitable grazing for several months to give his foot growth a kickstart; it may be worth giving up your riding in the short term to gain long-term benefits. The traditional Irish remedy to speed up slow growth is to graze horses on water meadows for six months and there may be more to this than hearsay. Water meadows provide a constant environment – and it is now thought that rapidly changing external conditions, now a fact of life with our unpredictable weather patterns, have an adverse effect on hoof health.

Following the same principle, there are now many topical products on the market said to help keep the hooves' natural moisture content in balance. Farriers tend to be the prime source of advice on what works best. When your horse is stabled, keep bedding as clean and dry as possible. Ammonia from urine and droppings is harmful both to hooves and to the horse's respiratory system.

Simply picking out your horse's feet before and after you ride and/or when you turn him out and bring him in helps keep hooves healthy. Bacteria tend to collect in the grooves on either side of the frog, which can lead to thrush. Good, regular farriery is one of the most important keys to improving poor quality feet and maintaining good ones. If necessary, look for a farrier who works closely with veterinary practices or takes remedial referrals.

Weak, crumbling horn can be a nightmare when you are trying to get a horse fit and keep him in peak condition, as shoes are inevitably lost or pulled off more frequently. Not only do you usually lose opportunities to work him whilst you wait for the farrier to come and put the shoe back on; you may find that the extra frequency of shoeing and making nail holes weakens the hoof still further, thus creating a vicious circle.

There are various answers to problem feet, ranging from nutrition to using 'hoof boots' instead of shoes or even, in some cases, working horses unshod: there is a growing enthusiasm for going barefoot and in the past year or two there have been a few eventers and even racehorses who have adapted well to this regime. However, it does not work for everyone and every horse and it demands a skilful farrier who under-stands exactly how he is shaping the foot and why (see Chapter 6).

For the majority of riders, shoes are still the norm even if hoof quality is poor. Again, breeds and types may have inherent strengths and weak-nesses: Thoroughbreds are notorious for having low heels and flat soles, which are prone to bruising, whilst Fell and Dales ponies often have hard-wearing horn that stands up to being worked unshod. Some owners opt for a mixture of both approaches and find that having their horses shod only in front works for them: they claim that the hind feet, which take proportionately less weight than the front ones, harden naturally over time and, of course, it minimizes risks if the horse kicks another one – or a person.

The bit between the ears

Getting a horse fit involves consideration for more than his physical well-being. He needs to be in the right mental condition, too, which involves everything from assessing his temperament (see Chapter 1) to making sure he is suited to and can cope with the job you are working towards and keeping him happy as an individual. This goes hand in hand with looking at your own temperament and capability. The majority of riders opts for geldings because they are usually, though not always, easier to train than stallions and mares. Both stallions and mares are entire horses and it is important that their use should be promoted in all disciplines so that breeding the next generation is based on actual performance as well as conformation and pedigree. The 'but', and it can be a big one, is that you are looking after and riding a horse who can be both enhanced and held back by nature, notably the reproductive cycle.

It is often said that only experienced, capable and empathetic riders should attempt to keep and/or ride stallions and that cannot be argued with. The old line that you tell a gelding, ask a mare and discuss it with a stallion has an awful lot of truth in it! Traditionally in the UK, stallion handling has been a male preserve, probably because at one time they were kept (often in conditions that would now be regarded as unfair) for breeding rather than performance; Thoroughbred colts might always have started with a racing career, but certainly the working life of a Flat racehorse is very short. However, as the call for proven performance lines developed, many women have proved themselves at least as good, if not better, than their male counterparts at establishing a rapport with stallions. There have always been ground-breakers, one notable example in the UK being international dressage rider, trainer and breeder Jennie Loriston-Clarke, who inherited the mantle of Catherston Stud from her mother, the gifted horsewoman Anne Bullen. Jennie competed at the highest international level on the stallions Dutch Courage and his son, Dutch Gold, whose bloodlines have been influential in dressage, eventing, showjumping and showing.

Whilst stallions are given respect, mares often get criticism; the word 'mareish' is an insult in itself. In many cases they are not as easy as geldings, but the right partnership between a good rider and a good mare can be unbeatable. Their breeding cycle can make them difficult at times in terms of mood changes and physical sensitivity and you may have to accept that if you have a mare, there will be occasions when she seems like the girl with the curl: when she's good she's very, very good, and when she's bad, she's horrid. Fortunately, advances in nutritional support mean that seasonal changes in behaviour can be minimized – what works for one mare may not work for another, so be prepared to try different feed additives. In extreme cases you may also want to ask your vet's advice about drug treatment, in particular Regumate.

All horses are individuals and riders who have the greatest success – in all disciplines – recognize this. Invariably, happy working horses of either sex are the ones who have interesting lives; most people would agree that this means allowing them a varied work schedule and plenty of time in a suitable grazing environment. There are those who say that their horses are not unhappy working in an arena nearly every day, but if you look at their work, these are usually event horses who do a mixture of jump-ing and flatwork and are taken to training gallops or other locations to do their fast work. Just as important, they get time in the field every day.

All horses and ponies can become bored if they do the same thing every day, which is why this book includes suggestions for groundwork, work over poles on the ground and gridwork. Some 'ploddy types' kept as hacks are ploddy types mainly because they are taken round the same two or three rides all the time; if they are given a bit of lungeing and ground-pole work and taken to different environments such as provided by sponsored rides, they brighten up enormously. Similarly, there are some very happy dressage horses at top level who go hacking and even jumping – and some who are probably not as happy. Many years ago I talked to a top rider whose horse was having a holiday; when I remarked that he was probably enjoying himself in the field, the reply was that he was far too valuable to turn out and his 'holiday' consisted of being moved to a large foaling box rather than his usual stable.

Hopefully, that attitude no longer exists. If you want more elevation in your trot, don't spend another hour in the arena – take your horse for a hack or a canter round the fields! And if you're frightened that he won't behave outside an enclosed arena, which is an excuse sometimes made, remember that the literal translation of dressage is training. Training a horse to listen to his rider in different environments pays dividends in all disciplines.

Science and common sense

You don't, of course, need to have a muscle biopsy carried out to determine whether a horse is going to be a top showjumper or an endurance horse. There are many factors involved in performing successfully, from physical characteristics to temperament and training. But understanding *why* a horse works makes it easier to select a potential mount for a given sport and to get and keep him fit for it. For instance, though any horse can take part in endurance rides at the lower levels, those at the top are invariably small and light, which makes it easier for them to regulate body heat.

It is important to pay attention to every aspect of management whilst you are getting your horse fit, including preventive measures that are often taken for granted – correct nutrition coupled with a healthy environment, an effective worming programme, vaccination against (at least) tetanus and equine influenza, good farriery, expert dental care and regular attention to saddle fit.

So why is understanding how your horse works so important, and how can it affect the way you keep him and get him fit? Some of the main reasons include:

● It can help you assess the job you are asking your horse to do, or to choose a horse whose physical characteristics help him find that job easier.

● It underlines why good management, routine care and preventive measures such as vaccination are essential.

● By knowing and monitoring your horse's physical baseline – such as his resting heart rate – you are more likely to spot signs of illness.

Environment matters

You can only build and maintain a horse's fitness if he is kept in a healthy environment. Over the past few years there has been increasing enthusiasm for keeping horses outdoors 24/7 and if you have enough well-managed grazing, with shelter from flies and biting insects in the summer and wind and rain in winter, or can provide a healthy environment in an outdoor pen or corral, there is no doubt that this is a fantastic system that benefits horses both mentally and physically. For instance, event riders say that New Zealand Thoroughbreds, who are kept out for all or most of the time because of the suitable climate, are usually far tougher and sounder than their British counterparts.

However, not everyone has this option and not all horses appreciate it. However loud the claims that horses are born to be outdoors, today's horses are domesticated and some of them grow to appreciate the shelter of a stable at times. It sometimes seems as if there is a school of thought which suggests that anyone who stables a horse for short periods is being cruel, but most horses seem happy on some sort of combined system as long as their routine and environment are carefully thought out and managed. There is also a big difference between keeping horses out day and night on free-draining, well-managed land and leaving them to

A well-managed field with natural shelter provides the ideal environment for 24/7 turnout.

Field shelters – either traditional or cross formation – are essential if natural shelter is sparse.

stand fetlock-deep in mud, looking and probably feeling miserable and tempting problems such as mud fever.

Having said that, there is no doubt that what used to be called stable vices and are now more fairly labelled stereotypical behaviour – weaving, crib-biting and wind-sucking – can affect a horse's soundness and there-fore his fitness and are directly related to being confined. Horses do not weave when they are turned out and although they may still crib-bite and wind-suck, the behaviour usually lessens. For these animals, it really is a case of indoors, in trouble and it is no coincidence that the highest incidence of stable vices will be found in Flat racehorses, who are usually stabled all the time they are not being worked. Some trainers, certainly in the areas of point-to-point and National Hunt racing, take a more enlightened approach and prove that a horse can be in the field for at least part of the time and still be in the frame. There are also some Flat trainers, such as David Nicholls, who make a point of turning horses out.

Stable design has a big impact on well-being, both in terms of respiratory fitness and the horse's stress levels – and sometimes, improving one can also help the other. For instance, most traditionally built stables have all the main openings – windows and doors – in the front, together with a ridge vent along the roof. By adding an extra window in the back wall, which can be closed if it becomes so windy that the horse cannot get out of the way of the resultant draughts, you not only increase ventila-tion but also give the horse another view. This makes a big difference to some horses, who presumably feel less penned in and become much more relaxed.

It is also important to remember that ventilation levels change according to weather conditions and building materials; in simple terms, a stable that is comfortably ventilated on a mild or even cold day with enough breeze to keep the air moving can become stifling and airless on a hot day with no breeze. Wooden stables are usually hotter than brick-built ones and roofing material also makes a big difference.

If you want to know exactly what sort of environment your stable provides, call in an expert such as one of the agricultural advisory service ADAS's equine consultants (www.adas.co.uk), who will carry out a test to measure the number of air exchanges and advise on how to make any improvements. Relatively inexpensive work can often make a huge difference.

A well-designed American barn at ILPH's Hall Farm with plenty of ventilation.

A physiological problem with stabling horses for long periods is that it can make them feel isolated from their neighbours. This affects not only their stress levels but their eating habits: if a horse can only see others on the yard if he has his head over the door and his forage supply is at the back of the stable, he may want to look out rather than eat (see Chapter 3).

RAO – the biggest threat

A horse can only be fit for his job if he can breathe properly. Threats to the respiratory system are far the biggest danger domesticated equines face, whether they be family ponies or four star eventers. This is not new knowledge; some twenty-four centuries ago Xenophon was the first horseman to write about what later became known colloquially as 'heaves' – from the 'heave lines' that became evident along the flanks when a horse's breathing became laboured. Later still the condition was labelled chronic obstructive pulmonary disease (COPD), but over the past few years vets and researchers have preferred the term recurrent airway obstruction (RAO), which describes it more accurately.

One of the most frightening facts about RAO is that it is estimated to affect up to 80 per cent of horses and ponies in many parts of the world. It is common in the UK and northern Europe. In recent times it has often been compared to asthma in humans. Some studies in human asthma point to dysfunction in the autonomic nervous system (see below), so the starting point of a major research project by Dr David Marlin and researcher Susi Norman was to ask if the same could apply to horses. Thanks in a large part to their work, vets now believe that RAO is, indeed, not simply a disease of the lungs, but a systemic or 'whole horse' condition which links to dysfunction of the autonomic nervous system (ANS). This system is different from the voluntary nervous system, which allows you to make voluntary movements, such as moving your arm. By contrast, the autonomic (or involuntary) nervous system is concerned with things you are not necessarily aware of. For example, it controls kidney function and, as mentioned earlier, the contraction and relax-ation of smooth muscle that aids the movement of food through the digestive system. It also controls the expansion and constriction of blood vessels and airways of the lungs.

Not all the blood vessels in the lung are open at the same time, but generally the airways are wide open. If you inhale something that might injure the lung, the body's defence mechanism is to close down the airways to prevent this happening – which works well until it reaches the point where they close so much it is difficult to breathe.

As the autonomic nervous system controls which and how many airways are open or closed, Susi Norman set out to discover whether it might not be functioning properly in horses with RAO. Her non-invasive study involved twenty-two horses; half were RAO horses free from clinical signs of respiratory disease whilst the other half did not have the disease. All were kept out all the time.

Dr Marlin said that investigating how the nervous system functions is quite difficult, even in human medicine. But one thing we can look at as an indicator is how the heart rate changes over time. Although we often describe the normal heart rate for a resting horse as being an average of between 35–42 beats per minute, in a healthy horse there are constant subtle changes in this related to what is going on in the autonomic nervous system.

The system itself branches into two types of function, sympathetic and parasympathetic: each uses different substances called neurotransmitters which affect heart rate modulation in opposite ways. In sympathetic function, adrenalin metabolizes slowly and leads to slow waves of modulation in heart rate. In parasympathetic function, acetycholine metabolizes quickly, which leads to fast waves of modulation.

To make things more complicated, horses who are naturally reactive, flighty or stressed have an increase in sympathetic function and a decrease in parasympathetic. To ensure that readings were not affected by the study horses' individual temperaments, behavioural specialist Dr Natalie Waran and Rachel Eager from the Royal (Dick) Veterinary School, Edinburgh, were called in to assess them without knowing any results of the work.

In most disease, such as heart disease or diabetes, the heart rate becomes less variable because the body is trying to adapt to the things that are not going well. As another example, if you look at a normal foal, the size and rate of the breaths he takes vary, but if there is a problem, he breathes faster and takes more regular breaths to try to get as much air as possible. Assessing heart rate therefore allowed the researchers to look at the horses' autonomic nervous systems. Using a non-invasive electrocardiograph (ECG) which was recorded by a computer, every heartbeat for a period of $1–1\frac{1}{2}$ hours was recorded in each horse. Because they were all relaxed and comfortable in their home surroundings and the work was carried out at the same time of day on each occasion, there were no outside stresses to affect the findings.

The results were fascinating. There was no difference in the parasympathetic function in the two groups, but there were wide differences in the sympathetic nervous function between the healthy horses. Those with high levels were the flighty, reactive types; while we know that the autonomic nervous system is affected by temperament, even when this was taken into account, there was still a big difference. However, in the RAO group, despite a wide range of temperaments, all the horses showed very little sympathetic control of heart rate.

Although it looks from this research as though there is probably a link between RAO and the autonomic nervous system, this is just the beginning of the story. Although we know what the clinical signs are, we still don't know categorically what causes the disease. We don't know if these horses are born with autonomic nervous system dysfunction and if so, whether it is a genetic problem. Alternatively, could it develop at the same time as the disease – or after they become RAO cases? However, because the autonomic system regulates the size of the airways, and these horses have problems with that, it is an area that will continue to be investigated.

Dr Marlin makes the point that many owners do not appreciate that RAO is a spectrum of disease. In extreme cases, some horses are so badly affected they cannot go anywhere near hay or straw; in less extreme but still severe cases, they show signs such as increased respiratory rates when put in stables, flared nostrils and nasal discharge and the rider of such a horse might find that he is reluctant to work and takes longer than expected to recover from exertion. This has obvious implications on fitness: pushing an unhealthy horse too hard on the incorrect presumption that he is lazy is unfair and potentially damaging. At the other end of the scale there are animals whose owners would probably never know they have the condition unless they are endoscoped and mucus is revealed in the airways. This is why many racehorse trainers and some event riders have their horses 'scoped' regularly; modern endoscopes are linked to video cameras, so the vet can see exactly what is going on in the airways.

At the time of writing, there is no alteration in how vets diagnose, treat and if necessary medicate horses with RAO and guidelines on clean-air management remained the same. However, ongoing research into ascorbic acid levels could mean there is also a nutritional part to the RAO

Rubber matting, with or without dust-free bedding, helps create a healthy environment.

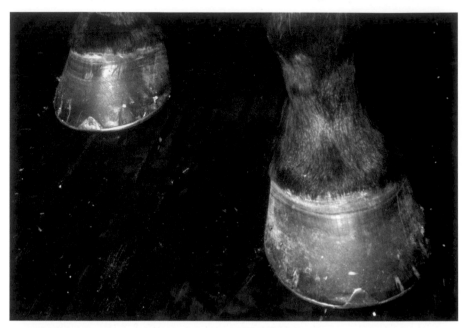

There are easy ways to improve ventilation in a stable.

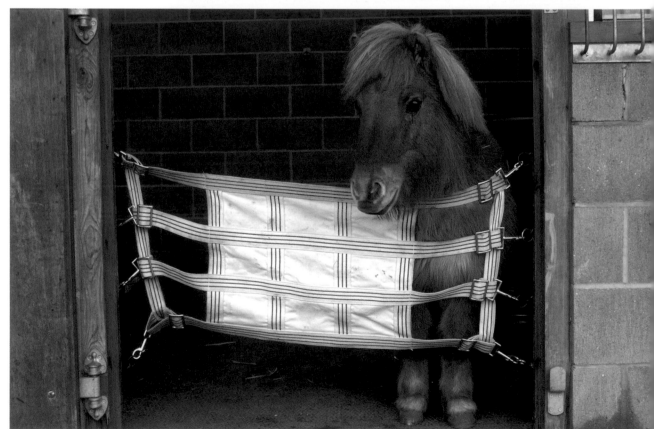

scenario. Ascorbic acid, or vitamin C, is an antioxidant present in the lung lining and plays an important role in mopping up oxidants or free radicals – naturally occurring substances which can cause cell damage and even damage to the DNA when found in too high quantities.

Guidelines for managing RAO cases make good practice for all animals, whatever their job. In terms of fitness as well as overall health, you should think about the following:

- When stabling is essential, so is a minimal dust and spore regime. Rubber mats can be used alone or with a small amount of dust-free bedding; however, even with materials such as chopped cardboard or shredded paper, you will get a small amount of dust in the environment from the horse himself and from tiny pieces of dried droppings, etc.

- Make sure the stable is well ventilated to allow frequent air exchanges, but at the same time, as free as possible from draughts. Never shut the top half of the stable door and if you are worried about your horse getting cold, add warmth through extra or more efficient rugs. Check stable design as mentioned earlier.

- Always take the horse out of and away from the stable to muck out and always muck out fully – the deep litter system is one of the worst enemies of respiratory health. Never groom a horse in the stable, as this throws dust into the environment.

- Feed haylage or soaked hay. Soaked hay only retains its benefits whilst it remains wet – see page 66.

- A minimal dust routine only works if your horse's neighbours are kept the same way. Your efforts will come to nothing if the horse next door is kept on straw or fed dry hay.

- If your horse lives out with a field shelter, follow the same guidelines for bedding and forage as in the stable.

3 Feeding for fitness

CORRECT FEEDING IS obviously essential for general health, but there are special issues to take into consideration when you are trying to improve your horse's fitness. There are also common misconceptions, so it is important to understand the basics of what you are trying to achieve and, if necessary, to get expert advice. Fortunately, this is freely available, as most good feed companies have nutritionists who can help you tailor an individual diet: obviously they will recommend products from their own ranges, but if you talk to several of the best-known companies you should find that whilst the names on the bags change, the principles behind them remain the same.

To get a horse fit, you will be increasing the intensity and/or the duration of exercise. Horse owners usually use the terms 'work' and 'exercise' to denote different things: work is most often thought of as achieving an aim, perhaps improving the horse's balance, whilst exercise is perhaps used in a context of getting rid of excess energy or 'stretching his legs' after the horse has been standing in a stable. Racing people may look at things differently and use the terms more as matters of degree – 'exercise' would cover road work and steady canters whilst 'work' covers the more demanding gallops. Perhaps it's better not to draw a distinction and try to make all 'exercise' productive, whether it is designed to improve balance and reactions or promote relaxation.

Whatever form of exercise your horse is asked to do, he needs energy and as the demands of his exercise regime increase – in terms of intensity, duration or both – so do his energy requirements. However, individual energy requirements vary enormously and horses who are natural 'good doers' will need less energy-giving food. Independent nutritionist Clare MacLeod gives, as an example, cases of horses who have gone round the

Badminton three-day event course on standard horse and pony cubes from a well-known feed company, and forage.

Feed companies generally formulate for the 'average' horse and there are plenty who don't fit that description, so it is important to tailor your horse's nutrition programme to his individual type and characteristics. As outlined earlier, it is also important to be realistic about the work that he is doing.

Another common mistake is to think that feed will produce fitness: this is linked to 'wishful thinking' feeding strategies, when a rider assumes that feeding a competition mix or cubes will automatically turn a horse into a competition animal. It won't: fitness is dependent not simply on energy supply, but on a training regime of gradual increases in exercise. Moreover, whilst feeding high-energy food won't, in itself, make a horse fit, if you are supplying more energy than the horse uses, you will probably cause behavioural and physical problems.

You also have to look at your horse's condition, as explained in Chapter 1. Energy is expressed in terms of calories and as we all know, an increase in stored calories leads to an increase in bodyweight. With an underweight animal, this is obviously desirable, but it is far more common for horses who are not fit to be overweight to some degree – and in this case, extra calories are the last things you want to supply.

This means that the often heard and often ignored advice that you should increase a horse's work before you increase his feed is more important than many owners realize. Upping the work before you up the feed can also help minimize the risk of rhabdomyolysis (commonly known as azoturia, or tying up) in susceptible horses, though this condition is now known to be more complicated than used to be thought.

Energy is not the same as nutrients. Energy in equine diets comes mostly from carbohydrates but also from fats and oils and protein, both in supplies previously stored in the horse's body and from his food. Another feeding myth to be ignored is that when you are getting a horse fit, you need to increase the protein levels of his diet – unless he is in exceptionally hard work, he does not need hard feed with a protein level of more than 10–12 per cent.

Don't get confused if you already use or are considering using feed balancers, which are fed in much smaller quantities than 'ordinary' compound feeds. Balancers are designed to provide nutrients in concentrated form and can be fed alone or as a top-up to a compound feed – in both cases, with plenty of forage.

Grazing and forage

One of the most important things to remember about feeding the performance horse is that good quality forage must always remain an important part of his diet. In most cases, it should be the main part; only racehorses and a few 'elite athletes' who are also good doers need to have some restriction on forage, which will supply calories but not all the necessary nutrients. Even then, it should never be fed at a rate less than 1.5 per cent of their bodyweight per 24 hours. When you realize that feeding to maintain weight means feeding, in most cases, 2 per cent of bodyweight, you see how important it is.

If you have a horse who gets fat at the first sight of spring grass, this can be a problem – particularly as being turned out to graze plays such an important part in keeping a horse happy. There are two strategies that can help, strip grazing and (if necessary and the horse accepts it), using a suitable muzzle such as the Greenguard design, which has special slots so the horse can still graze, but can only take in a limited amount of grass. Strip grazing is easy to maintain; set up the area you intend to use with temporary electric fencing, then graze it down with unaffected animals before turning out your potential fatty.

Forage should always be of good quality, free from dust and mould spores. This means either soaking hay or feeding haylage. Nutritionists now recommend soaking all hay in clean water as a matter of course. It is no longer recommended that hay should be soaked overnight, as it has been found that this leaches out the nutrients. Instead, most experts advise soaking for a quarter of an hour to two hours, depending on the quantity of hay and how densely it is packed together. Some owners shy away from haylage when feeding good doers, but as so many producers now make haylage in different energy levels, this is no longer necessary.

If you do have to limit the amount of forage given to a stabled horse but want to avoid him standing for long periods without eating – which won't do him any good either physically or mentally – you can use a small mesh haynet or use two ordinary nets at the same time, one inside the other. Reducing the size of the openings means it takes longer for him to pull out the contents.

A haynet with small mesh slows down the feeding rate and is especially useful when feeding haylage.

Feeding and fitness strategies

When you are starting a fitness programme from scratch, there is no reason why your horse cannot begin early slow work on a diet consisting mostly – or even wholly – of good quality forage. In other words, you can ride him off the field and – depending on the time of year and therefore the nutrient value of the grass – give him extra forage if necessary and add a feed balancer or broad-spectrum vitamin and mineral supplement.

People often worry about bringing horses in and riding them, because it has been drummed into us that we should wait for an hour after they have been fed before riding. This advice, though, is based on the traditional method of keeping horses stabled and feeding infrequent meals with a high untreated cereal content. Modern feeds are formulated with a much higher fibre content and although they still contain cereals (notably oats and barley) these are micronized – cooked at a high temperature – to make them much more digestible. Findings from the world of endurance riding, where horses are fed 'on the run', have led many experts to believe that as long as you haven't fed more than 1 kg (2.2 lb) of compound feed, it should not cause problems if you leave a shorter interval between feeding and working. However, it is important – as always – to warm up gradually and to use your common sense: going for an hour's hack in which the first half hour is spent in walk, half an hour after your horse has finished his feed, is very different from planning a fast work or jumping session.

The horse in true moderate to hard work will have increased nutrient requirements, mostly for the antioxidants vitamin E and selenium and for the electrolytes sodium chloride and potassium, so talk to your feed company nutritionist as you increase your horse's workload. Hard-working muscles produce waste products, including substances known as free radicals. These can be absorbed by antioxidants, thus helping to prevent tissue damage. Electrolytes play a vital role in combating dehydration – see Water and Electrolytes later this chapter.

It is often said that as horses go into really hard work, they lose their appetite and become 'picky feeders'. Traditionally, many owners have accepted this as normal, as they also accept increased irritability and bad temper as normal, but most experts now say that these signs should be investigated rather than ignored as they are often a sign of gastric ulcers. Research has shown that a frighteningly high number of competition horses have gastric ulcers; the latest research points to around 80 per cent of racehorses in training and up to 50 per cent of competition animals being affected. Diet and management are the overriding causes: although there is a heartening increase in the number of riders who realize the importance of turnout and forage, there are still top-class equine athletes who have long periods without eating and are given inadequate fibre.

Horses who are stabled have a physical and mental need to chew forage, as it is the nearest we can offer them to their natural grazing behaviour. Mentally, it may lessen the incidence of stereotypical behaviour such as crib-biting and wind-sucking and physically, it stimulates the production of saliva. Because horses are by nature trickle feeders, they produce a constant supply of acidic digestive juices to break down anticipated food. Digestion starts when the food is chewed and mixed with saliva; saliva counters acidity when produced in sufficient quantities but as horses – unlike other mammals such as dogs or people – can't salivate in anticipation of food, they need a continuous supply of forage. The need to produce saliva is another reason to ensure that your horse has proper dental care, as anything that compromises his ability to chew also compromises his ability to produce it.

For some reason, there are valuable feeds which some owners either ignore or dismiss when they are trying to get their horses fit. One is soaked sugar beet, which is not only an excellent source of digestible fibre but also palatable. If you have dismissed it because you don't like having to soak traditional beet pellets for 12–24 hours (depending on the manufacturer's instructions) and/or are worried about it going sour in hot weather during a prolonged soaking period, look at the new generation of beet feeds. These need only 10 minutes soaking, so can be prepared fresh for each feed.

Soaked sugar beet is a good, palatable source of digestible fibre.

Dried grass is another valuable and underrated feed. Fed dampened, either alone or mixed with other feed, it satisfies the need to chew, slows down the horse's eating rate and – because it is so light – can be fed in large volume. Alfalfa is another highly palatable, high-fibre feed, though it provides a higher level of nutrients.

Although we now know much more about the science of feeding, we can't use it to produce miracles, despite some of the advertising and marketing strategies! Nothing will turn a reactive, 'sharp' horse into a patent safety, or a 'plod' into a ball of fire. However, there are strategies which can help.

With the sharp, explosive horse, you have the comfort that in most cases, the fitter he gets, the more level-headed he will be. Similarly, the plod will usually become more energetic as he gets fitter simply because he will become leaner and less of a 'paddock potato'. Although diet will not change a horse's basic characteristics, it may help you to minimize problems.

Sharp or sensitive horses may also be difficult to keep condition on, particularly if they become stressed or excited by experiences such as travelling and competing. You may find that feeding slow-release energy sources such as soaked sugar beet, high-fibre feeds and oil helps you to keep this type of animal on an even keel. There are several types of oil suitable for feeding to horses, such as corn oil, vegetable oil from mixed plant sources and soya oil. There are also commercial additives in pellet form with a high oil content.

Magnesium, also, has been implicated in promoting a calm temperament; although most researchers are still saying there is no scientific basis for assuming that magnesium has a beneficial calming effect, there is plenty of anecdotal evidence to support the view and at least one company is already marketing a coarse mix with higher magnesium levels. You can also buy magnesium supplements to add to your horse's feed. It is beyond doubt that magnesium has a number of important functions and since in some areas soil is known to be deficient in magnesium, this will affect the nutrient quality of grass and hay.

If you want to give an energy boost to a laid-back horse, quick-release energy sources are often recommended – in particular, bruised or rolled oats. However, the success rate from this strategy is probably far lower than feeding slow-release energy feeds to the sharp horse – and if, as is sometimes suggested, you feed high-energy feeds you are also feeding more calories. In most cases, this is the last thing that you want to feed to a laid-back horse.

One thing that does not work for horses and should not be attempted because of associated health risks is glycogen loading. This is an idea that has come from the field of human athletics; it is an attempt to improve performance by increasing glycogen stores in the muscles, thus delaying depletion during the concerted effort of competition. Human athletes follow a programme which starts with hard exercise combined with a low carbohydrate diet, followed by several days of light exercise and a high carbohydrate diet. Their aim is to reach a stage where muscle fibres have higher than normal glycogen stores. If this is attempted with horses, there is a huge risk that the horse will be put at risk of contracting laminitis, or tie up.

Water and electrolytes

One of the often repeated golden rules of feeding is that clean, fresh water should be available at all times. It's something we often pay lip service to without really appreciating just how vital it is; not only does water constitute a major part of the bodyweight – around 65 per cent in an adult horse and even higher in growing youngsters – but even a small amount of dehydration can have drastic results on performance. It has been shown that a dehydration level of just 2 per cent will adversely affect a horse's performance; to put this risk into perspective, the pinch test, which is the commonest method of assessing hydration, will not show up a 2 per cent shortfall.

Although it is often said that a horse will drink an average of 27–36 litres (6–8 gallons) of water per day, this is only an average. In hot, humid conditions he could need three or four times this quantity, which is why it is important to ensure that he has a constant supply. It also means that it is important to know how much he is drinking; the drawback of automatic waterers, which are used in many large yards to save labour and time, is that it is usually impossible to assess how much an individual horse is taking in. It is much better to use water buckets or containers, which must be kept clean.

Empty, clean and refill stable water buckets at least twice a day. Water becomes tainted with ammonia from urine and faeces in the bedding and some horses will refuse to drink until they have become very dehydrated. If a horse seems reluctant to drink in his stable, it may be because of where the buckets or containers are sited. Research has shown that some horses are more ready to drink from containers mounted off the ground.

It used to be common practice to take water away from a horse for an hour before exercise, but this is no longer recommended and it is now accepted that if water is always available, a horse will only drink what he needs. The only exception may be just before a race, but opinions vary even on this. In some racing yards, it used to be – and in a minority may still be – standard practice to remove water three or four hours before a race. The faulty reasoning behind this is the belief that there is an increased risk of colic if the horse drinks too near a race or competition, coupled with the erroneous belief that if he does not drink, he will be lighter and therefore faster. In fact, water is emptied rapidly from the gut and is unlikely to sit there making the horse either uncomfortable or too far above his racing weight.

Dr David Marlin, a leading researcher into the effects of heat and humidity on horses (see Chapter 6) says that he would rather start a competition or race on a fully hydrated horse than on one who weighed 10 kg (22 lb) less but was dehydrated. He pointed out that endurance riders let their horses drink at regular intervals throughout work and competition without ill effect – though the water must not be ice cold, because this might cause constriction of the blood vessels of the digestive tract and consequent problems.

Riders in most disciplines now follow the example of endurance riders and offer their horses small, frequent drinks when working, competing and travelling. In human athletes, this has been shown to improve performance in some cases by almost a third. If your horse is reluctant to drink, particularly away from home, there are various strategies that might help; again, see Chapter 6.

The type of fodder you use will often affect the amount a horse drinks. Haylage or wet hay may result in horses drinking less than those fed dry or dampened hay. It has to be said, though, that even the best quality dry hay contains dust and mould spores. Soaking hay for between 10 minutes (for a small net) to an hour for a larger quantity removes dust and causes spores to swell so they do not affect the respiratory system. The catch is that this preventive measure only works if the hay is eaten whilst wet: as soon as it dries out, the threat returns. The old advice that hay should be soaked overnight is now generally agreed to be unnecessary and even counter-productive, as it also leaches out the nutrients.

It is also important to soak each batch of hay in clean water. If you re-use water, you are soaking hay in contaminants. Similarly, when you travel your horse, don't hang haynets for the return journey on the back of your trailer or horsebox as they will be exposed to everything from car waste products to dirt flung up from the road.

Whilst it is agreed that all horses need extra salt (see next section) the question of electrolytes (salts broken down into their chemical components) can still cause disagreement amongst vets and nutritionists. Some say that ordinary salt on its own is sufficient and that commercial electrolyte products are a waste of money; however, they now seem to be in the minority and isotonic electrolyte solutions are used as standard to rehydrate a dehydrated horse. The logical argument in favour of giving electrolytes is that horses do not sweat them out in the same percentage in their sweat as remains in their circulating fluids; if they did so, the levels would stay in balance. However, this doesn't happen: a horse's sweat is more concentrated in electrolytes, or hypertonic, so sweating produces a net loss of electrolytes.

If you have had a bit too much of a good night out and enjoyed a few too many drinks, try the sachets of dehydration salts available from any chemist and you'll see what a difference they make! Electrolyte solutions are invariably offered in water and it is essential that the horse is always offered plain water alongside it. There are many commercial electrolytes available and you may want to get advice and recommendation from your vet.

Sodium chloride is just one of the electrolytes in the body – the other main ones are potassium, calcium and magnesium – but it is very important and most commercial feeds and forage are salt-deficient. The old guidelines about the amount of salt a horse needs have been revised upwards: independent qualified nutritionist Clare MacLeod recommends two 50 ml scoops per day and points out that horses, unlike human athletes, lose huge amounts of salts in their sweat.

Supplementary benefits

The feed 'supplements' market is huge, as becomes obvious when you walk into any feed merchant or saddlery shop. Whether all are as essential as the manufacturers would have us believe is open to discussion, but there is certainly no such thing as a product that will turn an unfit horse into a superfit athlete. Although the term 'supplements' is widely used, strictly speaking, there is no such thing: under EU regulations, they have to be called complementary feeding stuffs or, if they can be correctly categorized still further, mineral feeding stuffs. In simple terms, they contain high levels of certain nutrients intended to balance the horse's diet and are fed in very small amounts with other feeds, including forage.

One reason for the tightening up of regulations is the minority of manufacturers who make unverified claims. There is a fine line between clever marketing and breaking the rules, but the Veterinary Medicines Directorate, an executive agency of DEFRA, says that any product which claims to treat or be able to prevent a disease must have a VMD marketing authorization. To get this, the manufacturer has to provide evidence that

Supplements should always be tailored to the individual horse and his job.

claims are justified. There are strict rules on terms that cannot be used unless a product has a VMD licence. For instance, it cannot be claimed that a product heals or even relieves a problem, which is why you will see many adverts containing phrases such as 'helps in the maintenance of healthy joints'. Phrasing of this sort does not mean that a product is not helpful, but it does prevent unsubstantiated claims. Semantics aside, there have been important advances in nutritional research that can benefit many equine athletes – and that, after all, is what you are trying to achieve when you get a horse fit.

For instance, as mentioned in the previous chapter, it is now thought that there could be a nutritional element to recurrent airway obstruction. Unlike humans, horses can synthesize vitamin C from glucose, but we know that levels are low in RAO horses. In a healthy horse, there is a balance of oxidants and antioxidants, but factors such as disease, environment or diet may upset that. Clinical trials have shown that dietary supplementation with a balanced antioxidant supplement may improve lung function both in horses who have RAO and healthy horses who are stressed – but it is not enough to simply increase the amount of vitamin C in the diet, and giving too much may actually result in poor performance.

The only addition that should be made to every horse's diet is extra salt, as explained earlier. Apart from the fact that most commercial feeds are deficient in this substance, they are otherwise formulated to provide suitable quantities of necessary nutrients if fed at the manufacturer's recommended daily amounts. However, this may be a minimum of 3 kg (6½ lb) per day and in many cases, particularly good doers and ponies, that would be far too much.

By the same token, feeding less than the recommended amount may mean that your horse is not getting enough vitamins and minerals. Feeding all or mainly forage, even though this is an excellent way of feeding as nature intended and keeping horses more content, will certainly mean that you need to fill in the nutritional gaps. In these cases, feeding either a broad-spectrum vitamin and mineral supplement or a feed balancer should do the trick.

Other supplements fall into four main categories: those designed to protect or improve joints and hoof quality, 'calmers' and products designed to help horses who crib-bite and/or wind-suck and may have gastric ulcers. All have devotees and all attract widely differing opinions!

Joint supplements

Supplements to protect and help maintain the horse's joints are widely used and many riders swear by them. Nutritional support has become the buzzword in all areas of horse health, but joint supplements are a particularly booming market.

The number of repeat sales suggests that many have a beneficial effect, but there is a bewildering number of ingredients and also conflicting views on what works and what doesn't. For instance, studies have shown that some substances which help when injected into the joint have no effect when given orally.

With many horses working and competing well into their teens, there is enormous interest in nutritional support for both helping and preventing joint problems such as arthritis. It's important to check whether products are formulated to try to prevent and/or slow down damage, or as anti-inflammatories.

Research into osteoarthritis comes from the human field, mainly because of the costs involved. This means that dosages for horses have to be extrapolated from those for people. This is generally accepted but what does raise problems is the question of effective substances. Whilst everyone seems to be confident that glucosamine is beneficial, it is in many cases combined with chondroitin sulphate – and Ian Wright is one of several vets who believe that it is a waste of time using chondroitin sulphate because studies show that it cannot be absorbed by the horse when given orally.

However, he says that reports have described positive effects of oral chondroitin sulphate in the management of human osteoarthritis. If, like many riders, you take it in conjunction with glucosamine to ease or try to prevent stiffness problems, you will probably benefit.

The commonest source of chondroitin sulphate is bovine trachea, another factor that makes some people uneasy. However, some companies say they use marine sources. Glucosamine occurs naturally in the horse and is used to help build healthy connective tissue in joints. Ian Wright says that though there is a dearth of studies in horses, it is the most logical choice for the treatment and prevention of equine joint disease.

There is also a lot of interest in MSM (methyl suphonyl methane), often described as a bioavailable source of sulphur. Sulphur is a mineral which is important for the formation of healthy connective tissue, but the horse is not well equipped to absorb it as a discrete substance. MSM is present in tiny quantities in many plants, including grasses, but extra supplementation is needed to try to help cases of osteoarthritis.

Dr Nick Larkins, a vet specializing in research and development, started using MSM in 1984 and introduced it into Europe. A friend of his who was an American vet reported good results in foals with joint problems who had previously been pretty much untreatable and Dr Larkins found that horses who were responsive to 'bute' were in most cases responsive to MSM.

Whilst bute can play an important role in the short term by reducing inflammation and discomfort, it is widely acknowledged that in some circumstances it can have side effects, including deadening the sensitivity of the horse's mouth and the possibility of causing liver damage. It is also a prohibited substance under FEI competition rules.

There is also growing interest in bromelain, extracted from the pineapple plant. Initial findings report that it has anti-inflammatory effects as well as speeding up tissue repair.

Some 'natural' anti-inflammatories have been used for hundreds of years and there are many herbal supplements formulated to give nutritional support for stiffness problems. However, 'natural' does not necessarily mean they can be used with impunity: if your horse is on medication, check with your vet in case using the two together could cause problems. Furthermore, herbs, like synthetic drugs, can also have contraindications. For instance, Devil's claw has many advocates, but because it stimulates the uterine muscles in mares and the digestive system it should not be used for pregnant mares or horses with stomach ulcers.

Other herbs and plants said to be helpful are willow bark, celery seed, meadowsweet, chamomile, yucca, grape seed extract and mint. Omega-3 and Omega-6 oils, enjoying a boom in human medicine in areas ranging from improving concentration to relieving depression, are also becoming increasingly popular for maintaining joint function.

Cider apple vinegar is one of the oldest remedies, for horses, dogs and humans. Dosage recommendations vary, so check with your vet if necessary.

Willow is a natural anti-inflammatory.

As always, read the small print when comparing supplements, as proportions of active constituents vary. For instance, Ian Wright says that extrapolating human dosage shows that a 500 kg (1,100 lb) horse needs at least 10 g glucosamine per day. The overall quantity of compound supplement given to achieve this dosage may vary from one product to another.

Whatever supplement you use, don't expect instant miracles. As Dr Larkins explains in relation to MSM: as we are providing conditionally essential nutrients – nutrients where normally there is an adequate level, but under stressful conditions such as osteoarthritis the demand far exceeds the normal supply – we have to expect a 'lag time' before the beneficial effects fully come into play. He describes the process as being rather like mending a wall which has a few lost bricks that need to be repaired or replaced. The good news, he says, is that rather than hide this problem with anti-inflammatories, we are providing the conditionally nutritional 'goodies' to help repair the problem and ensure that it becomes no worse. Therefore, the horse benefits not only in the short term but also for the long term, as this problem (which is not reversible) is reduced to a minimum.

Hoof supplements

Over the past few years there has been a lot of research into how nutrition can help improve poor quality horn, resulting in the marketing of many specialized feed supplements and balancers. Whilst a healthy horse on a well-balanced diet – which must include high levels of good quality forage – should have better feet than a malnourished one, it is now acknowledged that some nutrients are especially useful.

Because horses are individuals, there are cases where what helps one horse will have minimal effects on another; again, it comes down to genetics. As Ian Wright puts it, you can supply the necessary nutrients but you can't guarantee that every horse will be able to absorb them.

With regard to this, it is also important to check that your horse can digest his feed properly, so dental care is important. If he can't chew his feed properly, he won't get the maximum benefits. Similarly, if he is a good doer, could he be missing out on basic nutrients? In this case, a good broad-spectrum vitamin and mineral supplement could be the cheapest way to put things right.

These days, few owners routinely feed bran, but it definitely should not be fed to horses with hoof problems. It is high in phosphorus and this blocks the absorption of calcium, thus creating a deficiency.

Whatever you try, don't expect to see any signs of improvement for eight to ten weeks – and remember that it takes about nine months for healthy horn to hit the ground. As with all supplements, it's important not to feed more than one at a time without getting specialist advice.

When reading the product labels, look out for the following ingredients:

- **Biotin** is a B vitamin which helps maintain a healthy periople and therefore a correct water balance in the foot. It is sometimes fed alone, at a dose of about 15–20 mg per day for a 500 kg (1,100 lb) horse, but more usually in combination with other ingredients. Most researchers now believe it is most effective if fed in combination with methionine and zinc.

- **Methionine** is often described as one of the 'building blocks' for healthy connective tissue.

- **Zinc** is implicated in the formation of healthy keratin, a material found in the outer layers of horn and skin. Defective keratin leads to crumbling hooves.

- **Copper, vitamin C** and **essential fatty acids** are also necessary for healthy hooves and can be obtained through diet or supplementation as necessary.

Calming supplements

Calmers are probably the most controversial supplements. Some swear by them whilst others believe their benefits are all in the riders' minds – because the riders believe that their horses are going to be more relaxed, they are less likely to be tense themselves.

However, there is increasing anecdotal evidence that some ingredients do have a beneficial effect on some horses. Magnesium (mentioned earlier) is often cited – and there is much anecdotal evidence to support it – as are herbs such as chamomile. Valerian, once a favourite component of many calmers, is now a prohibited substance under FEI and Jockey Club rules, so competitors should read labels carefully.

Products to alleviate gastric problems

As mentioned earlier, many cases of gastric ulcers are thought to be linked to too little forage and too much high-starch food, and management techniques may also be implicated. Horses who show signs of stereotypical behaviour, in particular, crib-biting and wind-sucking, may also experience discomfort linked to gastric problems: it is no coincidence that the highest incidence of stereotypical behaviour is found in racehorses who are stabled most of the time.

In the past few years, a number of products said to neutralize stomach acid have been developed and marketed, but these should not be looked on as a substitute for better management with more turnout. These products are claimed to help reduce some cases of crib-biting and/or wind-sucking and bring together new science and old beliefs. Prof Daniel Mills, Royal College of Veterinary Surgeons' recognized specialist in veterinary behavioural medicine, details a Victorian 'remedy': horsemen would put bark, a lump of chalk and a lump of salt in the horse's manger. The bark was to increase the fibre in the diet, chalk was an antacid which buffered the acidity of the stomach and salt increased salivation, which also reduced acidity.

Staying within the rules

As all areas of equestrian sport come under close scrutiny, competitors need to be vigilant that they do not break rules concerning forbidden substances. The FEI's veterinary committee says that it is not against certain substances which are naturally present in the body and used on a preventive basis – so the many leading riders who use glucosamine supplements are, for the moment, on safe ground. However, the FEI is targeting the use of injected medication, non-steroidal anti-inflammatories (NSAIDs) such as hyaluronic acid and will be keeping a watching brief – not to act as a police force, but to protect horses' best interests. It advises that any competitors who are worried about whether or not they can compete legally using a particular supplement should consult their vets. If a vet does not have the definitive answer, this should be available from the appropriate ruling body.

Case history

Showing producer's fitness regime

Lynn Russell is a top show producer and dealer who specializes in cobs and hunters. She is renowned for spotting potential in horses to whom most people would not even give a second glance – nearly all of her horses come from Ireland and often arrive thin, hairy and having had little or no handling. Visitors to her yard often see a scruffy new arrival and ask: 'What on earth is that?' – and when they see him at his first show, cannot believe he is the same horse.

Showing producer
Lynn Russell.

Lynn's successes are too many to mention and she has been dubbed 'the queen of the cobs' because she is so successful at finding and producing them. Champions who have come from her yard and whom she has produced from scratch include Cosmic, Satellite, Draco, Triangulum, Milky Way, Apollo and Polaris and she has also had a host of champion show hunters such as Wishful Thinking, Bailey's Pukka Tukka and Bailey's Over Ice. She is as talented riding side-saddle as she is astride and has had numerous successes not only on hunters but also on cobs – usually the last type of horse to be thought of in terms of this discipline. One of her greatest achievements was to win the British Isles championship in the year of the Queen's Silver Jubilee riding Polaris, her champion heavyweight cob, side-saddle.

Lynn is renowned for her hard work and determination and her ability to get the best out of any horse. Sometimes, such as when she was badly injured by a kick from a horse, she has needed every last bit of these qualities. Showing is a discipline that comes under heavy fire for the number of overweight horses competing and Lynn is insistent that her horses must be well covered with muscle, not fat.

Lynn won the British Isles championship riding her heavyweight cob, Polaris, side-saddle.

Another victory, astride.

LYNN RUSSELL

Fitness philosophy

A show horse has got to be relatively fit because when you are competing regularly you have the stress of travelling and long days. Often you're leaving early in the morning and not getting home until night. A horse or pony who isn't fit gets very tired travelling, because they have to stand and brace themselves against the movement of the lorry no matter how carefully it's driven. Also, when you get to a show there's a lot of activity going on: it might seem like a peaceful sort of existence, but today's county shows throw out a lot of challenges for a horse to cope with – as well as the crowds, banners and so on you might have to cope with everything from bouncy castles and funfairs next to the ring you're competing in to motorbike displays and parachutists dropping in from the sky!

Horses can use up a lot of adrenalin and if they're not fit, they can 'die' on you in the ring. A show class doesn't in itself maximize the horse's athletic ability and stamina, but there is a lot of standing around coupled with bursts of energy and he must be in a fit condition to cope with this. Sometimes a horse will be at a show and unable to relax fully all day – or even longer, if it's a two-day show and you're staying away. They don't lie down on the lorry and they don't usually lie down in temporary show stables, because there's always so much going on around them.

Getting a horse to the right stage of fitness for showing is very different from, say, getting him fit for eventing. The event horse needs to be what I would call ultra-fit, because he has to do long periods of hard, fast work and needs to be in different bodily condition. There's been an awful lot said about fat show horses, some of it true, some of it untrue. The main problems come because a show horse has to be well covered to present the right picture, but he must be covered with firm muscle, not fat.

Over the years, show horses have come in for a lot of criticism. Some of it's justified, some of it isn't. A lot of people don't understand the difference between muscle and fat. If you get hold of a horse's crest, move it and feel it's firm, that's muscle. If it wobbles and moves from side to side, that's fat. If you can stick your finger into a horse's neck or hindquarters and lose it, that's fat! When I'm judging, I sometimes get on horses and look down to see two spare tyres under my knees. That's fat on the shoulder and it's the most difficult place to get rid of it. A show horse should be toned and muscled and you should be able to see good muscle definition.

You also have to remember that in showing, unlike any other discipline, the horse is ridden by the judge: an unfamiliar person has to get on and assess his way of going and the ride he gives in $1\frac{1}{2}$–2 minutes. Obviously schooling plays a vital part in making sure – or trying to make sure – that the judge gets a good ride, but fitness is also a key element. You can get a horse too fit and there's a fine line between having him just right and slightly over the top, so he's too quick on the uptake.

Feeding

I buy all my horses from Ireland and they often come in very poor. They've probably never been wormed, vaccinated or had their teeth seen to, but before you can start putting that right you need to give them a few days to relax and get used

Horses who arrive at Lynn's yard in poor condition get small, frequent feeds.

before they are offered the next feed. Although I routinely feed haylage, because it isn't easy to buy decent hay, I start them off on hay – sometimes haylage is too much for the system. As the horse starts work and begins to build up, I gradually increase the energy level of the feed, though I make sure that the diet is still based on fibre.

I turn horses out a lot. You don't want to start pushing food through their system and cause azoturia or laminitis. It isn't necessarily over-feeding that can cause these problems, but also changes in diet. I accept that there are still some show horses who are much too fat, but the problem isn't universal, as some people would have you believe. Unless they're youngstock or need the grass, I tend to turn them out on bare fields and feed hard feed, because that way I know what they're getting. They don't get too fat, but being turned out keeps them sweet. Some sharp horses are out day and night – with the right rugs and hoods they're absolutely fine even when they're fully clipped – and others are out in the day and in at night. You can get a horse perfectly fit from the field as long as you feed and worm him correctly.

to a new environment and to recover from the journey. If you worm them straight away, it can bring on an attack of colic, so I wait until they're eating and drinking properly.

Getting weight on a 'hat rack' isn't a case of throwing loads of food at him all at once. You have to give small feeds at frequent intervals – the old rule of 'feed little and often' applies in all cases, but especially this one. When you don't know what they've had but suspect it might be very little, you don't want to flood the system with all sorts of nutrients all at once.

I start them off on a high-fibre, non-heating diet and offer four or five small feeds a day. If they leave anything, it's always cleared away

Schooling and fitness

Depending on a horse's strength and condition, I'll probably start by hacking him out quietly to strengthen the muscles. Once he can take a little more, I'll often introduce work on the lunge using the Pessoa system – this is designed to encourage the horse to work from behind and helps to build up the topline. When it's used correctly, it helps build up the horse's muscles and encourages him to carry himself in a good outline without forcing it.

It takes a year of proper feeding, proper worming and proper schooling to get a horse fit and ready for a full showing season. People who see horses when they come in here often can't believe what they look like three months later, but to me it seems to take forever. It's really satisfying, though. I've always made horses from scratch – I've never wanted to go out and buy a top-class made horse, even if I could have afforded to.

Showing horses is unlike any other discipline. Your horses are ridden not just by you, but by a judge who is unfamiliar with them and has to assess how they ride in 1½–2 minutes. That means the horses have to be fit enough to cope with the stress of travelling and long days at shows, but not too sharp on the uptake. There's a very fine line between the two.

I know I take a different approach from some people in that I work them throughout the winter, whilst other producers may turn them away after the Horse of the Year Show ends the season and don't bring them up again until January or February. I prefer to keep my horses in regular work, because I think it maintains their fitness. They all get a short break when they need it and they get turned out, but they do a mixture of hacking out and working in the school on good going until the end of February/beginning of March, when hopefully the weather starts to change for the better. Sometimes you have to be very hopeful, but you can't do much about that!

By that time they're in good body shape but not too fat, covered and muscled. That's when I let them down a bit: I might change their feed from one I've used to build them up to a diet that's higher in fibre and lower in protein. I'll

turn them out more and though I still work them, it'll be on the basis of 15–20 minutes in the school then all day or all day and all night out in the field, depending on the individual horse.

Once I feel I've reached the right stage of condition and fitness, I'll keep them on maintenance levels of food and work. That's why I like to do a lot of the early shows, because when you bring out novice horses you have to keep the balance right. They have enough energy and stamina to cope with early competitions without being thrown straight into the hurly burly of the full-blown circuit.

I'll school a horse for as long as it takes (but in appropriate increments) to get a result: if he's going well, that might be just 10–15 minutes. If he behaves badly, I'll take him in the school for very short periods, several times a day. With a difficult horse, I don't do long sessions: it's much better to do a short period of work and get a bit of a result, then reward him by stopping and bring him out again later. I'll sometimes do it four or five times a day – I think the record is seven sessions in one day! It's better to score points than to start a war and it also gives you time to re-think your strategy and the horse time to settle down.

Each day you work a horse, he should go a little bit better. If he hasn't had enough work when you've achieved your result, ride him in the field or go for a hack. A lot of people over-drill their horses and the result is that the horses become resentful. Horses have to enjoy what you want them to do – you have to keep their brains in good shape as well as their bodies.

It's the same with teaching people. Sometimes you're best with a short lesson, sometimes it takes a bit longer. When people get tired, they ride badly. 'Little and often' means you start and finish on a good note.

Lynn keeps schooling sessions short, as she does not believe horses should be over-drilled.

leg too far back, you get a horse going sideways because he thinks that's what he's been asked to do. Different horses have different jobs: mine have to walk, trot, canter and gallop in balance, be forward-going but come back when they're asked and be athletic and supple.

I want my horses to work correctly all the time, except of course when they're being allowed to relax. Even when they're out hacking they must walk out properly and go in an outline; I might ask them to bend to the left for a few strides, then go straight, then bend to the right for another few strides to keep them supple and listening. My horses have to learn to go in the correct way all the time: I'm not carrying the horse, he has to carry me, and also the judge.

I often use brushing boots when I work them, but not when I turn them out unless there is a particular reason for doing so. Boots can slip and rub if you leave them on for long periods in the field. I don't trot horses on the road except in an emergency; I don't agree with the theory that trotting on hard going hardens the legs. In my view, all it does is subject them to unnecessary concussion. Horses do enough tearing about on their own in the fields, so why add to the risk of them getting splints and other problems when you don't need to? In fact, I try not to trot on hard going at all.

Show horses, with the exception of show hacks, have to show the ability to gallop, but they should lengthen their stride, not go like bats out of hell for three circuits of the ring. We have to teach horses to gallop, but we don't do a lot of fast work: it will be short spells, not long periods. We're on clay soil, which gets boggy and rutted,

Once you've got the work established, you have to continue maintenance schooling so the horse understands exactly what you want. Sometimes people say I look as if I'm not doing anything in the ring, but because I've spent so much time at home saying 'This is what I want, this is how I want you to go', the horse understands what his job is and how he has to go not just for me, but for the judge.

You work a horse and get him fit for the specific job he has to do. For instance, I don't do lateral work because if you get a ride judge who is not quite as balanced as he could be and puts his so we don't gallop in the field in the winter because of the risk to their limbs.

As soon as we have good going I do as much schooling in the open as possible. If a horse doesn't understand what is asked of him when you want him to lengthen and go on, or isn't naturally forward-going, I take him out with a seasoned horse who knows how to do it – but I don't do too much, or they learn how to anticipate, and that can cause real problems in the ring. You see a lot of hunters and cobs who have got ring-crafty and take off from the corner.

Rider fitness

My own fitness is very important and I take it very seriously. I've had a couple of serious accidents and on both occasions, doctors told me that if I hadn't been so fit and had good muscle tone, the damage would have been a lot worse and it would have taken me much longer to recover. I have to admit that my recovery time has also been down to sheer stubbornness!

In 2002 I was standing watching a horse who had just arrived from Ireland being ridden in the school. Someone called out to me and I turned to answer them and at that moment and for no apparent reason, the horse shot backwards and double barrelled both hind legs. I was in the wrong place at the wrong time and broke all my ribs down the left side of my body and ruptured my spleen and kidney. I was in intensive care for a week and in hospital for three weeks; I came out feeling – and looking – like death and rode at the Horse of the Year Show six weeks later.

The fact I was able to do that was partly down to physical effort, but a lot of it was down to my mental approach. I didn't want to let down either

my horse or my sponsors. When I work a horse, I have a goal: I say I want to get this horse to the Royal International Horse Show and the Horse of the Year Show this year, or next year. In this case, I said I was determined to ride at the Horse of the Year Show, though no one thought I would do it and I think a lot of those that said they believed me were actually just humouring me. I wasn't being stupid, despite what people told me: I wouldn't have considered it on a horse I didn't know, but this was Polaris, a horse I knew inside out and I knew if I could get there, he'd do his best for me.

When I came home, I worked with a personal trainer for six weeks – he was a man in his sixties who was really fit and supple, which was an inspiration in itself. I told him what I'd done and what I was trying to achieve and he designed a special programme for me to improve my weak areas: I also lost half a stone, and there wasn't much of me to start with.

I got to the Horse of the Year Show and after that worked in a gym for six months, building strength and stamina slowly. I've got a treadmill, so I worked on that, on an exercise bike, with light weights and doing exercises such as push-ups. I ride four to eight horses a day as routine and also do all the yard jobs – mucking out, filling and carrying haylage nets, doing water – which means I'm on the move, bending and stretching for most of the day. I do the same as the girls who work here; we work as a team and I don't ask them to do anything I don't do myself, plus I have to do all the other work connected with a dealing business.

Keeping yourself and your horses fit isn't easy, but it's important. You have to want to do what you do to put the effort in.

4 Fit to start

Whatever you are intending to get a horse fit for, whether it is a 16 km (10 mile) pleasure ride or a three-day event, you will be building a pyramid. At the top of the pyramid is the time at which you intend to have your horse in peak condition and at the base is your starting point. To get there, you will be working on three different areas: cardiovascular fitness, strength and suppleness, all of which complement each other to produce, hopefully, an equine athlete. At the same time, you will be trying to keep your horse contented, thus paying attention to his mental fitness.

To get a horse fit, you gradually increase the stress on his body so that his response to it improves. If done correctly, this will not cause any harm; stress does not have to be a dirty word. You can't get a horse, or a human athlete, fit without increasing stress – if you keep the workload at the same level all the time, the level of fitness will also remain static.

The time it takes to achieve basic fitness – which, as a rough guideline, should enable you to complete a Pre-novice horse trials comfortably – varies according to the age of the horse, his type or breeding and how fit he has been in the recent past. For this reason, the guidelines in this chapter, which deals with establishing basic fitness, can only be seen as a general framework. It would be wonderful if you could say that on week 1 you will do precisely this, on week 2 you will do exactly that, until you get to week 8 and can be guaranteed to have a horse ready to compete. Unfortunately, it doesn't always go exactly to plan.

The young horse who has been backed and ridden on for a year but is now being got properly fit for the first time will need longer than an older horse who, for instance, has been kept ticking over during the winter and is now being prepared for a spring competition season. And

It is remarkable what can be achieved by a steady, well-constructed fitness programme. These two pictures show Harry, in the condition in which he was admitted to the ILPH, and (below) being ridden out after rehabilitation.

although generalizations can be dangerous, cold-blooded horses such as cobs and those with a high percentage of draught blood nearly always take longer to get fit than horses with more Thoroughbred or Arab blood. Modern Warmbloods have a higher percentage of Thoroughbred blood than in the days when a top dressage rider famously described the German team's horses as 'dancing elephants' and they may be the equivalent of three-quarter Thoroughbred or even more – but though they have become a force to be reckoned with in eventing, top riders say they still need more time than the full Thoroughbred.

Riders who are preparing for top-level competition, such as three-day eventing, plan their fitness programmes so that their horses peak at a given time: if you're a Pippa Funnell or a David or Karen O'Connor, you'll tailor your programme to the season so that your horse peaks for the big events, as it's no good running at Badminton, Burghley or Lexington with a horse who needed another week's work to be at his best. As you can't keep a horse permanently at peak fitness, you also factor in the need to reduce his workload to the maintenance level appropriate for the job he is aimed at so that it can be built up as appropriate for the next challenge in the calendar.

However, as most of us will never ride round Badminton or compete in a desert endurance marathon, we should be able to reach and then maintain a reasonable level of fitness in our horses without the need for such fine-tuning. That doesn't mean we can take fitness for granted; if demands of work and/or family or enforced lack of opportunities to ride in winter means a horse's workload is reduced, it's important not to fall into the trap of assuming that he can do nothing all week but eat grass and then do a Riding Club horse trials or go showjumping every weekend. There are horses who are asked to do that and some manage it remarkably well, but they stand a much better chance of staying sound and performing better if they have a more consistent work programme.

A horse who has previously reached the level of fitness you are aiming at will retain much of it if he has a short break of a month to six weeks and is either turned out all the time or, preferably, kept in light hacking work. Although many riders like to give their horses short breaks – or may have no choice if, for instance, a horse suffers a minor injury – giving long holidays lasting several months is, in general, no longer a popular choice as it means starting from scratch when you start work again.

The inevitable question is 'How long will it take to get a horse fit?' Because horses are individuals and owners' routine and other commitments vary, exact times will vary. However, if everything goes according to plan and there are no setbacks along the way, you will be looking at around eight to ten weeks to get a mature horse who has been got fit before and whose schooling is established, but is starting from scratch after a lay-off, to the stage where he is ready for a Pre-novice horse trials. In fact, riders in most disciplines work to a similar timescale; when you start competing, you will be able to judge from your horse's performance and recovery whether you need to increase his fitness, or maintain it.

The young horse who is being got fit for the first time, especially the one who has just been backed, is more difficult to assess. He has so many new experiences to cope with, from the very fact of being ridden to travelling and seeing new sights and sounds, that it really does pay to go slowly and you should keep in mind that he will not be truly fit for a year to eighteen months after he has been backed. Young horses will usually find new experiences exciting, which can fool their rider into thinking that they are fitter than they really are – but half an hour of bouncing around at his first show may be followed by a sudden drop in his energy level and there can be a fine line between achieving your object, whether it be a dressage test, a showing class or a showjumping round, and having to push a tired horse. It pays to remember that overtired four-legged youngsters can be like overtired two-legged ones: fractious and stroppy!

One thing you will not find in these pages is a selection of neat charts or graphs instructing you to do carry out a particular type of work on day 1 for so many minutes, followed by a similarly detailed programme for day 2, up to day 56, with every minute detailed. As explained earlier, you can follow general guidelines but you can't get horses fit by numbers: apart from the fact that every horse is an individual, you also have to factor in the time and facilities you have available and variables such as whether you have access to slopes and hills.

The best approach for the average owner with various other commitments is to work through stage one and then try to plan a week ahead at a time so you can keep variety in your horse's work. This will allow you for instance, to lunge for 20 minutes on a day when you are short of time and do half an hour's schooling and a three-quarter hour hack when more time is available. It also means you won't be tempted to beat yourself up because The Fitness Programme says you should be doing X and you have a meeting that overruns or a child who comes home from school with a sickness bug. Life happens, and fitness work has to be fitted in around it!

Before you start

Before you put your horse or pony into work, check that he has his equivalent of an equine MoT test. His worming and vaccination programme must be up to date and he should have had a dental check and any treatment necessary. In the case of the young horse, this may include removing wolf teeth. His feet and shoes should also be in good order.

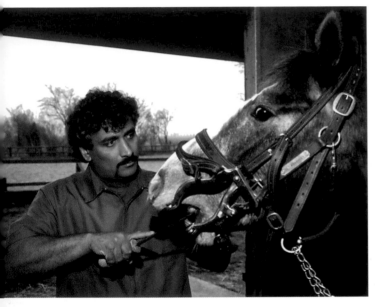

Regular dental care is essential for all horses and ponies.

Depending on the time of year, you may want or need to clip your horse at some stage. The best approach is usually to clip when you need to, not merely to make him look smart, as leaving coat on his back and loins will help keep his muscles warm when you are doing basic slow work. Even if you are faced with the combination of a dense coat and mild weather, you should be able to get away with a minimal clip: taking the hair off the underside of the neck and chest is often enough.

Tack and equipment checks

Before you put your horse into ridden work, check your tack, as the horse in 'soft' condition is more vulnerable to rubs. Little preventive measures can make a big difference: using rubber discs on your bit and/or applying petroleum jelly to the corners of the mouth can prevent the skin rubbing or splitting and soft girths with an element of stretch throughout their length are better than ones with no 'give' or with elastic inserts at one end. Apart from the fact that girths with elastic at only one end can encourage saddles to slip to the side on horses with round barrels, they do not 'give' as evenly as the horse breathes.

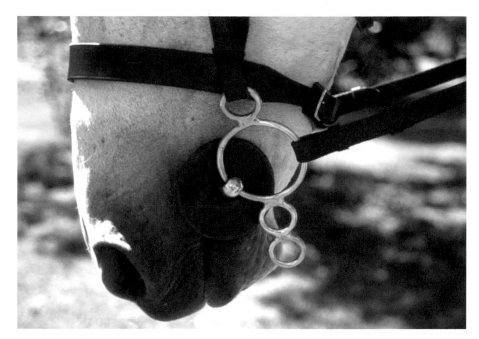

Rubber bitguards can help prevent the corners of the lips being rubbed or pinched.

Elasticated girths with inserts at both ends (as ringed), or those with stretch throughout, are better than those with no 'give', or with inserts at one end only.

Saddle fit is just as important when you are starting out as when you are ready to compete, yet a surprising number of riders use any old saddle for basic fittening work or assume that the saddle which fitted when the horse was in a leaner, harder condition will also be fine even when he is a different shape. Unless you are confident that you can assess it yourself, it can be an investment to get your saddle checked by a good fitter as you are about to start work; he or she will be able to see if it needs adjustment and suggest a rough date for a re-examination.

Don't make the mistake of assuming that this absolves you from being able to recognize when you are heading for problems – you need to be able to see when professional help is required and it won't necessarily occur in neat annual or six-monthly slots. Fine-tuning saddle fit and accommodating horse and rider's needs is a skilled job, but realizing when a saddle is about to cause problems so that you can get help is not difficult: you don't even need special knowledge to be able to do it; just be observant.

The best approach is to check your saddle once a month – perhaps more often if your horse is losing weight or muscling up – and at any time when you suspect things might not be quite right. For instance, if your horse suddenly starts tensing or stepping sideways when you saddle him, or feels as if he is humping or dropping his back when you mount, or raises his head and tenses through his back when you go into rising trot (when excessive movement of the saddle will be more obvious) then get checking.

You should also check whether he is showing signs of discomfort as part of your daily grooming routine. Is his back soft, especially behind the withers and under and just behind the saddle seat area, or does he tense or flinch when you run your hand along his back with firm but consistent pressure? See Chapter 10 for more hands-on information and techniques.

Although we tend to think of the horse's back as strong, because it looks as if it conveniently designed to take a saddle, he is as susceptible to back injury as we are – probably more so, considering what we ask him to do whilst bearing a rider's weight. In fact, a top saddle fitter once described the art of saddle fitting to me as a 'damage limitation exercise'!

The saddle which rests on your horse's back comes into contact first with the skin, which is obviously covered in hair unless the coat has been clipped off in this area – which is not recommended. The thickness of the skin varies according to the breed or type: native ponies and horses with a large proportion of cold blood have thicker skin than Thorough-breds, for instance. Skin is bonded to connective tissue called fascia and underneath that are the muscles.

The largest mass of muscle and one particularly vulnerable to damage from ill-fitting saddles is the longissimus dorsi, which is situated under the saddle. The trapezius muscle behind the withers is also vulnerable, especially from saddles which are too narrow in the tree, and pinch. The vertebrae and dorsal spinous processes – wings of bone – are underneath the longissimus dorsi; the vertebrae are actually much lower down in the body mass than many people imagine and the only parts of the spine you can actually feel are the spinous processes.

Although injuries to bone structures from ill-fitting saddles are fortunately rare, those to the skin, fascia and muscles are all too common. They can range from bruising and muscle spasm, usually caused by saddles which are ill-conformed for the horse's back or badly fitting, to girth galls and skin infections resulting from lack of care and/or hygiene – inadequate grooming or tack cleaning can cause an awful lot of problems.

A well-fitting saddle is one that fits the profile of the horse's back, does not interfere with his movement and distributes the rider's weight over as wide an area as possible. It does not follow that because a saddle is expensive, it will be a good buy: no matter how prestigious the name or whatever the quality of the leather, if it doesn't fit horse and rider it is a problem waiting to happen.

Using a flexicurve to assess the tree width needed – the white hairs are signs of damage from badly fitting rugs.

Assuming that your saddle is in good order, with a sound tree, and that (if it is flocked with conventional flocking) there are no bumps or unevenness, it can be checked on the horse. If you spot any problems, don't use it until it has been professionally checked or you could be setting up long-term damage. Never risk using a saddle if you have the slightest suspicion of a twisted or damaged tree; the former is often caused by riders who mount from the ground and pull on the saddle as they do so, which is why it is sensible to mount from a mounting block whenever possible, whilst trees are often damaged if saddles are dropped or if a horse falls or rolls whilst wearing a saddle.

When you put the saddle on, make sure it is not placed far too far forward: saddle fitters say that many of us don't allow for the fact that as a horse moves, his scapula rotate back about 7 cm (2¾ in). Check that the tree width is still correct for the horse's shape – and be aware that this can change dramatically and quickly. Viktor, the young Warmblood in the photograph, matured and muscled up so much as a 3- and 4-year-old that if his owner had not had a Wow modular saddle with air flocking that could be continually adjusted, she would have needed to change her saddle at least twice.

A young Warmblood, Viktor, as a 3-year old. He matured and muscled up so much as a 3- and 4-year-old it was just as well that his owner, Donna Houghton, had an adjustable, air-flocked Wow saddle.

If a saddle tree is too narrow, it will pinch on either side of and below the withers and if it is too wide, it will press on and just below them. Your saddle should also follow the contours of the horse's back; a saddle built on a tree with a pronounced dip to achieve a so-called 'deep seat' will only fit a horse whose back dips correspondingly.

If you are checking an existing saddle that started off as a good fit, you need either someone observant on the ground or a rider who is about the same height and weight as yourself. With the rider on board, look for the following and if you don't find them, get help:

- The saddle should be level from front to back and the rider should be balanced, neither tipped backwards nor forward.

- When viewed from behind, the saddle should sit evenly. If it is over to one side, is it because the rider pulled it over when mounting or because he or she has uneven stirrup leathers and is therefore putting more weight in one stirrup than the other? Alternatively, does the rider have a possible imbalance and sit crookedly, or is the horse's musculature uneven?

- Still standing behind the horse, check that the saddle is clear of the horse's back all the way along the gullet, especially under the rider.

- The panel should be in contact with the horse, but the pommel and cantle should not press down on the withers or the back. It is often said that you should be able to fit three fingers between the pommel and the withers and the cantle and the back, but there is a certain amount of leeway – and there are times when it will be impossible to achieve. The amount of clearance needed also depends on the work the horse does: jumping usually calls for greater clearance than flatwork. Even saddles marketed as 'close contact' must have sufficient clearance. As a rough guide, when the rider stands in the stirrups, the helper should put one finger between the pommel and the withers. If the finger gets pinched whilst the rider is in this position, the saddle will come down too low when the horse is working.

If it's so far, so good, horse and rider should move off, warming up gradually and working evenly on both reins. Watch out for any signs of tension or discomfort, such as a restricted stride or the horse swishing his tail or putting his head up – they may or may not be connected to saddle fit, but it is one of the options to explore. Watch the way the saddle moves, too: you will always get slight movement, but do not want to see noticeable rocking, whether from side to side or backwards and forwards.

These guidelines apply to all types of saddles except treeless ones, which are a different proposition. Although the jury is still out, many authorities feel that some of the better ones have a lot to offer and certainly their adaptability makes them an option not only for horses who are difficult to fit but also for those who are changing shape. My experience has been that many horses go well in a range of treeless saddles designed by Heather Moffett, a classical and remedial trainer who founded the Enlightened Equitation organization.

With conventional saddles, the Flair air system has much to recommend it. Personally, I have found that every horse or pony I have owned – including Connemaras, Thoroughbreds and horses with broad backs and virtually no withers – have gone better with the Flair system fitted in their saddles rather than conventional flocking. However, as with every system it is only as good as the person who fits and adjusts it.

The design of saddle has a big effect on your security and, when doing fitness work, even pure dressage specialists will find they are better off using a general purpose saddle, as it allows you to ride short enough to

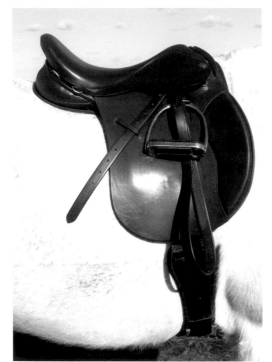

A general purpose saddle that is not too forward cut can be used for flatwork, exercise canters and jumping.

canter with your weight just off the horse's back. It will also give you more security if your horse spooks or throws a buck. It does not have to have an exaggerated forward cut – there are some excellent modern saddles marketed as VSD, or very slightly dressage, that even the most dedicated straight-legged dressage aficionado will feel happy in!

It is also important to make sure that the saddle fits you – and again, a knowledgeable fitter can help solve many problems. Few of us are symmetrical, thanks to general wear and tear and problems caused by, for instance, sitting in front of a computer for most of the day. Whilst most riders are aware of the need for the horse to be comfortable, our own balance and physical well-being must also be looked at – see Chapter 11.

Rug fitting is also important; a lot of owners don't realize the problems ill-fitting rugs can cause. When horses develop white hairs at the withers, which replace hairs that have been rubbed off, many riders assume that the saddle is to blame – it can be, but more often than not, rugs are to blame. A horse may wear a rug for many hours at a time, so if you get even a slight pressure point, the pressure is applied for such a long period that the resulting damage can be worse than many people realize.

Rug manufacturers claim that most problems are caused because horse owners often buy a size larger than they should, under the mistaken assumption that the more it covers, the better. In fact, if you use a rug that is too long, the proportions will probably also be wrong and no matter how well made, how high-tech the material or how expensive it is, it will slip back and put pressure on and around the withers. This in turn can restrict the horse's movement: imagine how you would feel if you spent all night with pressure on the back of your neck and shoulders.

So remember the basic guidelines: a standard rug without a built-in neck cover should lie 5–10 cm (2–4 in) in front of the withers when fastened and the back edge (incorporating the top of the tail flap if one is included) should reach just to the top of the tail. The cut should allow for free movement of the shoulders when moving; if your horse has a pronounced slope to his shoulder and the stride that goes with it, he may be more comfortable in a design with shoulder gussets. There should be enough room at the front for you to be able to fit two hands' widths between the secured chest fastenings and the horse.

If the design is well cut for your horse's shape and the rug is the correct size, it should stay in place when the horse gallops, lies down and rolls without the need for cross surcingles or under-belly harnesses being done up tightly; you should be able to fit a hand's width between the cross surcingles and the horse and harnesses should be adjusted according to the manufacturer's specifications. Cross surcingles incorporating a small degree of elasticity allow a little 'give' as well as providing security.

It should be easy to find rugs to fit animals with reasonable conformation. However, as many are designed for 'average' animals of half-bred type, there may be some who are a little harder to cater for. Cobs are the obvious example: their broad chests mean that rugs which are theoretically the right length often don't meet at the chest, but if you buy the next size up, the neck will gape and the rug will pull back onto the shoulders, causing pressure and rubs. The best solution in this case is to buy a chest expander, a rectangle made from tough rug material with fastenings at each side that take the corresponding fastenings on the rug, or to have a rug made to measure – many rug companies will do this at relatively small extra cost.

There are also companies who have analysed the conformation and proportions of many different breeds and designed rugs accordingly. For instance, there are now many rugs suitable for larger ponies and for deep-bodied horses.

Do you need extra control when you are about to start a fittening programme, especially if you are putting a horse into slow work who would rather be going faster, or starting out with one who thinks the best way to liven up walk work is to find things to spook at? In general, it is sensible to use a martingale for faster fittening work, as this will give you extra control and the benefit of a neckstrap if you need one. Neckstraps are not to be sneered at, especially on young and/or forward-going horses who want to be one gear ahead of their rider's choice and can end up jogging and swinging their quarters sideways. Slipping your fingers under the neckstrap and applying a short 'pull and give' is often an effective method of getting a horse to slow down and can act as a half-halt, thus helping you rebalance him, without putting undue pressure on the reins and starting a pulling contest.

Running martingales are most commonly seen and, if fitted correctly, will only come into play when the horse raises his head above the angle of control. Rather than follow the textbook advice of gauging fit so that the rings reach the withers when pulled back, adjust it so that when the rings are taken along the underside of the neck, they reach the gullet. This method seems to work even if the horse has a slightly straight or particularly sloping shoulder, which can affect the usual fitting method. Obviously any method can only be a guide and you may need to alter the fit slightly when you start riding, but it is better to have the martingale slightly loose than too tight and you definitely do not want to see a kink in the reins. If your horse tries to grab at the rings, switch to a bib martingale, which will make this potentially dangerous habit impossible.

Standing martingales can give extra control on novice horses, as they work on the nose – the control point the horse is accustomed to right from the start of his education. Again, they should be fitted so that when pushed up to the underside of the horse's neck, they reach the gullet; if necessary, they can be a hole shorter than this.

The Mailer bridging rein, designed by showjumping trainer Carol Mailer, is a new idea that many riders will find very helpful. Simple but effective, it in totally non-restricting but prevents the reins being pulled through your hands and also encourages you to ride with your hands as a pair.

The Mailer bridging rein can give the rider more control without imposing artificial restriction.

Checks and safeguards

When you are getting your horse fit, it is important to minimize the risks and spot any potential problems as soon as they arise. This means being continually observant: if your horse comes out one day feeling slightly stiff or dull, don't ignore it. He could be tired because he worked harder than usual the day before, or he could be feeling uncomfortable or even incubating a virus.

Experts such as Dr David Marlin recommend that every horse should have his temperature taken daily, at the same time. A horse will show a slight rise in temperature before, for instance, he shows any clinical signs of a virus – and Dr Marlin says that if you stress a horse when he is incubating a virus, it can double the time you need to get him back to normal.

Other simple measures include basic ones that we can all be guilty of neglecting when we are in a hurry. Check before you start work – are his shoes secure, or is one coming loose? Lose it when you're in the middle of a canter session – or even in walk in the school – and you could end up with a puncture wound or bruised sole that will keep your horse off work far longer than the wait for the farrier to refit it.

Do you feel your horse's legs and feet before and after working him each day? If he comes out with three cold legs or feet and signs of heat in the fourth, check first of all that he is sound when trotted up and on a circle. If you have the slightest doubt, at least give him a couple of days rest and if you have the slightest suspicion of a tendon injury or laminitis, get veterinary advice immediately.

If he already has acquired lumps or bumps such as splints or windgalls, do they remain stable or do they suddenly become hot or increase in size? Again, ask your vet's advice. The same applies if a young horse starts developing a splint, which will usually be painful when pressed.

Equal caution and attention should be paid to the way you start and end your work sessions once you have graduated beyond the walk only stage. It is essential to warm up and cool down and if the horse is amenable, starting and finishing with 10 minutes of walk work is always a good idea: when hacking, follow the old maxim of 'Walk the first mile out and the last mile back.' Whether hacking or schooling, it may be

Always allow time to warm up and cool down on both reins.

appropriate to use an exercise sheet in some conditions; some riders like to use a magnetic therapy rug for 20 minutes before and after work (see Chapter 10).

For the superfit horse who is in true hard work, ready to race or compete in a three-day event, research shows that spending up to 20 minutes in trot after hard exertion helps to prevent the build-up of lactic acid. This can again be followed by a cool-down period of walk. Some yards use horse walkers to carry out pre-work walking, but they should be looked on as an aid to work, not a substitute for it.

The general programme

Stage 1

No matter what your eventual aim, you need a solid base on which to build and this is always the same: long, slow distance work, commonly referred to as LSD. This does not mean that you are aiming to become an endurance rider, nor is it a new idea; traditional hunting grooms brought their horses back into work after a summer at grass by spending six weeks in walk, beginning with a few minutes each day and building up to 1–1½ hours daily before introducing periods of trot. It was a conservative programme, but though many people would now say that six weeks in walk is unnecessary, it achieved the desired effect.

Depending on your horse's starting point, you ideally need to think of spending two to four weeks in walk, gradually building up the time. Unfortunately, horses do not read fitness programmes and in some cases – especially if you have to do your walk work by hacking out on the roads – getting on a horse who has not been ridden for a while and asking him to restrict himself to a quiet half hour's walk may be laughable or, in the worst scenario, dangerous. If he is going to play the fool, then for safety's sake, you may have to lunge or loose-school him for a few minutes and allow him to get rid of excess energy; by doing this in an enclosed area on a safe footing, you can at least minimize the risk of him slipping. A few days of this, making sure to spend an equal amount of time on both reins, should help to get his brain in gear enough for you to begin ridden walk work.

Whenever you work a horse in a school, whether you are lungeing, loose-schooling or riding, take into account the surface (see Chapter 6.) Deep going, in particular dry sand, requires a lot more effort from the horse than a wetter or firmer surface, such as the increasingly popular combination of rubber granules and sand. Even then, the size of the rubber particles may make a difference: some trainers believe that smaller particles give a better footing and are less slippery than larger ones.

Different riders in different disciplines have their own views on the use of protective boots when building fitness and also the most appropriate types, but it's sensible to start off with a well-designed set of brushing boots to protect against knocks. These, like any numnahs or saddle pads, should be washed frequently to avoid the risk of rubs and skin infections.

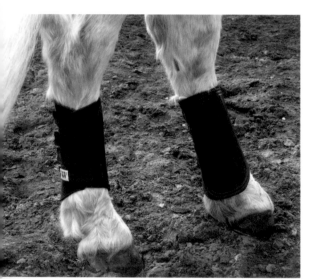

Brushing boots can be a sensible precaution.

It is often recommended that horses should wear knee boots for roadwork, but these can sometimes cause as well as prevent problems. Keeping them in place means fastening the top strap tightly, which can rub or even restrict movement.

The best approach is to tailor the boots you use according to your horse's balance, the way he moves and surfaces to be encountered. For instance, if he is at the gawky, clumsy stage and feels as if he is literally going to fall over his own feet, then knee boots may be advisable when riding on the roads. If he over-reaches – which young horses sometimes do through lack of balance – overreach boots are an obvious precaution. Exercise bandages are, in general, not recommended except in special circumstances: they may support the tendons if put on correctly, and as such may be a safeguard on a horse who has had a previous tendon injury, but if applied unevenly they can cause more harm than they prevent. If your horse has had a tendon problem in the past, ask your vet's advice about preventive and protective measures.

Depending on the weather conditions, you may also want to use an exercise sheet when doing slow work; some of the best modern designs are waterproof and breathable. If you are riding on the road, then fluorescent, reflective equipment is essential even in daylight. At the very least, riders should wear tabards. If brushing boots and exercise sheets are fitted, high-visibility designs offer extra protection.

The quality of the walk is important. It needs to be active and rhythmical without being hurried and it should certainly not be a case of slopping along and admiring the scenery. The horse does not need to be 'on the bit' in dressage terms and working too hard at this may be counter-productive, as you will be asking unfit muscles to hold a shape for which they are not ready. Instead, aim to have the horse stepping actively into a light, elastic contact with the nose slightly in front of the vertical.

Use high-visibility equipment when riding on the roads, even in good weather.

In an ideal world, you would start off doing half an hour in walk, building up to 1–1½ hours a day. In real life, doing half an hour's walk for many people may mean riding up the road for 15 minutes and then turning round to come home, which is a good way of teaching a horse to nap. If you don't have a short, circular route, you may have to do a couple of days initial walk work in the field or in an arena and then start off with 45 minutes to an hour's roadwork. However, there is nothing to prevent you getting off and walking the last 15–20 minutes home – and think how it will help your own fitness!

This stage of fitness training can be much easier if you have access to a horse walker as this enables you to build up the initial walk work safely: most horses, even those who are likely to stage their own firework displays under saddle when they start work, behave sensibly on them. As with lungeing or loose-schooling, it is important that the horse spends the same amount of time on each rein to make sure that the muscles are worked evenly.

Stage 2

When you have built up comfortably to an hour's walk exercise per day, life becomes more interesting for you and your horse. By now you will probably be at week 3 to 6 in your programme, depending on how long you spent in the initial walk work. You can now start riding large figures in the school – 20-m circles, three-loop serpentines, changes of diagonal – and, depending on the stage of your horse's education, introduce exercises such as leg-yielding and shoulder-in to add variety and build athleticism.

You should also be able to start short periods of trot, both out hacking and in the school. Think of an easy, rhythmical working trot, balanced but not hurried. If you live in an area that gives you access to gradual inclines, trotting up these will help because your horse will be encouraged to use his hind legs. If you live in a totally flat area, you can follow the same guidelines at this stage but once you have been through the next stage and introduced canter, you may want to follow a system of interval training to compensate for the lack of hills.

Whether or not you trot on the road depends on which school of thought you follow and what the roads are like in your part of the world: reading the views of riders in the second part of this book may help you make up your mind and if you have a good vet who knows your horse and what you are trying to achieve, it is also worth asking for a professional opinion. One of the most common philosophies is that trotting on level roads with a good surface is better than trotting on a rutted track, but in recent years there have been problems in many parts of the country with new road surface materials that have proved treacherous for horses.

Lungeing in walk and trot, spending an equal amount of time on each rein, can become a regular part of the regime if necessary. Start with 5 minutes on each rein and build up gradually to 10 minutes; see Chapter 8 on ways to make your lungeing more effective and less boring for the horse, but be prepared for the fact that some individuals with a sense of humour, especially native ponies, will always let you know that they consider trotting round in circles to be a mindless occupation. Make sure that you keep your circles large, preferably working to a 20-m diameter, as small circles put strain on the joints. If you need more control, forget the standard advice about remaining still whilst the horse makes a circle around you and walk a small circle; this enables you to keep a shorter lunge line and have greater influence over the horse's way of going.

Stage 3

If all has gone according to plan, you should now be able to introduce short periods of canter work on good going, which usually means in a school and out hacking as long as the ground is neither too hard nor, conversely, deep and heavy after rain. But whilst it's important to be sensible, it is also easy to become over-protective, so use your common sense – the ground doesn't have to be perfect, but it should have a bit of 'give' and you should avoid obvious dangers such as hard going topped with a slippery surface after a long period of dry weather followed by sudden rain. Common sense also suggests that you should not canter in

A balanced canter on good going.

the same place every time, even it if presents the only decent bit of going on a hack, or your horse will start to anticipate. That might not seem a problem until a change in the weather suddenly turns good going into bad and you are arguing on slippery or rutted ground with a horse who says, 'But we always canter here.'

The quality of the canter is important; it must be balanced and rhythmical. This applies to competition as well as fitness work, especially in eventing: a lot of riders go fast over the ground but get time penalties because they are not keeping a rhythm. Letting a horse gallop on between fences is pointless if you then have to waste time fighting to slow down so as to set him up for a fence. Since this also requires greater effort from the horse it is counter-productive in two respects. When a horse canters in a balanced rhythm, he breathes in time with his strides; this, as mentioned in Chapter 2, is known as locomotor-respiratory coupling. As the forelegs come down after the moment of suspension, the internal organs move forward against the diaphragm and air is pushed out of the compressed lungs. As the head is raised again, the internal organs are pushed back and the lungs can take in more air upon inhalation. If the horse breathes properly in rhythm with his stride, it is very efficient for him, but if he breathes out of rhythm, he has to work a lot harder to breathe and therefore becomes tired more quickly.

It might be tempting to think that fitting studs to your horse's shoes will make him safer and enable you to do more work on less-than-perfect going. However, a lot of farriers still recommend that studs should be used only for competition – and then for extra security rather than allowing you to compete when conditions should really dictate otherwise – and that using them all the time gives a false sense of security and can even add to jarring of the limbs (see Chapter 6.)

Prolonged cantering on the lunge is not recommended, because of the strain it imposes on hock joints in particular. When you are building fitness, it is better to work on straight lines to start with: and when you are working on accuracy and balance through canter transitions, it is better to do it under saddle rather than on the lunge, as you can dictate the size and number of circles and use the whole of the school or schooling area.

At this stage, or the next, you may need to rethink your tack. If faster work in the open makes your horse excited, you have to make sure that you are always in control and it is better to use a different bit or nose-band or something like a Market Harborough or a Mailer bridging rein than find yourself getting tanked off with or dumped. A correctly fitted Market Harborough works wonders on the horse who tries to throw up his head and go and because it is brought into action (and therefore also immediately released) by the horse rather than the rider's hands, it is far less likely to cause problems than some training aids.

At one time, it was standard practice on many yards – particularly show-jumping ones – to always send horses out hacking in draw or running reins, but these can cause so much damage they really cannot be recom-mended. Apart from the fact that they can leave muscles tired and ligaments stretched, few riders have the skill to release them as soon as the horse responds, which is counter-productive. It is sometimes said that there can't be anything wrong with them if riders like John Whitaker use them, but the answer to that is – can you ride as well as John Whitaker?

Whatever you plan to do with your horse, you could find that preparing for and competing in an appropriate level of dressage competition will give you something to work for and an idea of how your horse reacts to the stimulus and challenge of travelling as well as the actual competi-tion. Travelling, warming up for 15–30 minutes depending on his individual needs and riding one or two tests should not cause undue stress at this stage, unless he normally competes at Medium level or above and has had a lengthy lay-off. In that case, the sensible option may be to compete hors concurs at a lower level, as you will be using competition as a fitness gauge rather than as an end in itself. (Competing hors concurs means that you will not break competition rules or be accused of pot hunting.)

Stage 4

You will now be ready to make increases in effort and duration of work. Depending on the horse and your aims, schooling sessions may become more frequent and more demanding; three or four schooling sessions a week can be combined with hacking, lungeing and pole work/gymnastic jumping and you can trot and canter up hills, if you are lucky enough to have some. Be open-minded: you may not want to jump seriously, but most horses enjoy gridwork with low fences and it is a good way of

Work over poles increases a horse's athleticism and adds interest to his work.

building suppleness and fitness. Even if you have a total aversion to leaving the ground, there is a lot you can do with pole work – for inspiration, see *Schooling with Ground Poles* by Claire Lilley (J. A. Allen) and also Chapter 9.

You should be finding that your horse feels stronger (in terms of endurance rather than harder to hold) and more supple than when you started. However, it is essential to remember the warming up/cooling down periods before and after each period of work and even when you are hacking, to start and finish with periods of walk. It is also sensible to follow a day when he has worked hard, perhaps because you have had a more than usually intense schooling session, with one where he works in a different way: go for a hack, combine a short hack with an easier schooling session or give him a day off to relax in the field. Grazing is one of the easiest ways to get a horse to lower his head and neck and stretch the muscles along his back, and he certainly won't complain about it!

To build cardiovascular fitness, you can now start lengthening the canter sessions, either in the field or out hacking, depending on where you have access to the best going. Even if you do not follow an interval training programme (see the next chapter) you can borrow from it by doing twice weekly sessions of 2 minutes in canter followed by 3 minutes in walk, repeated three times. As your horse's recovery rate improves, build this to 3 minutes in canter followed by 3 minutes in walk, again repeated three times. The canter you are aiming for is rhythmical, energetic but not extended – if you have a stopwatch and can mark out 400 m distances on reasonable going, aim for a speed of 350–450 m per minute.

When you are working comfortably at this level, you should have achieved a basic level of fitness and your knowledge of your horse and the way he feels and recovers from work will tell you if you have reached your goal or need to improve. If you want a more precise knowledge of his fitness you will need to use a more scientific approach, such as proper interval training – but it cannot be stressed too often that whatever fitness philosophy you follow, you must be able to assess your horse as an individual, not just in terms of a graph or chart.

Case history

Fitness pointers for a young eventer

Jo Lawrence has wide experience of breaking, schooling and competing young horses, including potential point-to-pointers, dressage horses, working hunters and eventers. Her first love is eventing and at the time of writing she is competing on her own horse, Gisyerand (Andy), a three-quarter Thoroughbred 8-year-old gelding who was given to her as a youngster by his breeders and who has needed time and patience.

Jo Lawrence and Andy.

JO LAWRENCE

Fitness philosophy

I was given Andy as a 4-year-old when he had done a bit too much in a school environment – he has a cheeky attitude and soon lets you know if you are not doing things the way he thinks they should be done. He had become quite nappy and a bit fed up with the whole 'riding thing' when I got him. I'm quite patient – some might say a bit too patient at times – but I think this was probably a good thing for a horse like Andy.

I spent a long time long-reining him at first and went for miles round my friend's farm, which probably helped get us both fit! It also helped to get him thinking forward and to trust me when I said 'go'. As soon as I could, I started hacking him out.

Thoroughbreds and three-quarter bred types like Andy can very easily fool you: he looks fit and may give the impression that he is fit before he actually is, so you have to be aware of their recovery rates. Also, once you start regular canter work they lose their 'belly' and the stomach line comes up, so you have to be careful not to assume they are fit enough just because they look more streamlined.

At first, young horses can't hold fitness. I believe it takes them until they are 7 to be able to do that, so you have to build up slowly. It certainly didn't help when Andy fractured a splint bone as a 6-year-old, and had to have a year off!

Feeding

It's really hard to buy good hay, so I feed ad lib haylage that is fairly dry. I like my horses to go out every day and if the fields are too wet, I have a small bark surface turnout area and feed haylage and carrots on the ground.

The rest of the diet is based on Simple Systems products and consists mainly of lucerne, unmolassed sugar beet and grass nuts. Andy also gets linseed, seaweed and brewers' yeast, plus salt and, when he needs them, electrolytes. He used to be very excitable at competitions and I have found the magnesium-based calmer, Nupafeed, to be a real blessing. It really levels him out and doesn't contravene any competition rules.

Jo's horse walker is used in addition to, but never instead of, a carefully thought out work programme.

Schooling and fitness

We moved to the East Anglian fens from a hilly area, so as a result I have to do more to get horses fit. That's when my horse walker is useful, though it's used as well as work, not instead of it. You don't have to spend a fortune if you are prepared to look round – we bought it second-hand and built the centre partitions and it stands on rubber matting which we bought from the local council and originally came from a playground.

I've been lucky enough to work on some great yards and to be around some wonderful competition horses and show ponies. During this time I got lots of tips and ideas on what I would do with my own yard if I was ever lucky enough to have it. Now I have, and have tried to make it both user- and horse-friendly.

The yard is very compact and I can see the horses from just about anywhere. They go out every day and when it's too wet to use the fields, which can become boggy because of the clay soil, I have a 20 x 40 m arena with a rubber and silica sand base and a 15 x 15 m bark-surfaced turnout area.

Jo's bark-surfaced turnout area means that horses can go out even when the fields are too wet.

Most of Jo's fittening and schooling work is done out hacking.

The best thing about living here, though, is the hacking – if I want to, I can go for miles without touching a road. I can also hack to Ely Eventing Centre, where facilities include cross-country fences of all sizes and descriptions, for lessons with Tina Ure. We hack two miles each way, which helps to warm up and cool down, then start on the flat before getting down to the fun bit of jumping. We work on keeping Andy settled

and use different exercises to get us both thinking. I did a lot of showjumping and working hunter classes in my early days and my natural instinct is to try to place a horse at a fence, but nowadays the idea is to keep a good rhythm and not look for a stride, which I find quite hard at times.

Once a month, we go to a local dressage centre for a lesson with Malcolm Brown, who is a List I dressage judge. This has been really rewarding and I hope that one day I'll be able to get the same standard of work in the dressage arena as over fences.

Because of the problems I've had with my other horse, I've learned that a good farrier is essential and Tim Murfitt has played a vital part in keeping Andy sound and fit. It really is a case of 'no foot, no horse'.

I do a lot of my fitness and schooling work out hacking, because it helps to keep horses thinking forward. One day a week we go out for 2½ hours and go for miles and the rest of the time we hack out for 1–1½ hours. I always walk on a loose rein rather than making Andy go on the bridle, to try to keep him relaxed as well as going forward. I'll pick him up to do our trot work, which would normally be for 8 minutes on fairly even ground.

For canter work, I can ride round a local reservoir. Twice a week, as part of my hacking, I will do a form of interval training – after he's loosened up, he'll do 3 minutes canter, 2 minutes walk, 3 minutes canter, then walk home. I'll be aiming for what I'd call a hand canter: not a strong canter, but stronger than the canter you would use in the school.

In an average week I'd probably only use the school once or twice for flatwork and jumping and I might also lunge: I'm not much of a person for gadgets, but I like to use a Chambon to encourage the horse to stretch over the topline and work from behind and I do lots of transitions. Andy works a six-day week and has one day off, though I never give him a complete rest day after a competition. I always walk him out on the roads and trot him up to make sure he is sound.

Twice a week, Jo incorporates a form of interval training into her hacking.

Every few weeks a friend and I box up and travel to the beach to do canter work there. The horses really enjoy it and the going is good; it's like running on good-to-firm, even ground without too much concussion and you can do your canter work and stand them in pools of sea water, which is good for their legs.

We walk out to the beach, which takes about 10 minutes, then pick up trot and go out in one direction on the harder sand, walking and trotting. This not only continues the warm-up, but means we spot any patches which might be slightly softer. We can then follow our tracks back in safety and incorporate a strong 5-minute canter before coming back to walk and cooling down.

We also try to go to the forest now and again for a change of scenery. I believe that you need to keep the horses happy in their minds as well as healthy in their bodies, and going to places in the lorry other than lessons and competitions is very good for this – for all horses, but especially for young ones.

Rider Fitness

I used to go to the gym regularly, but now I never have time. Riding and all the normal horsy chores like mucking out keep me fit, though. I also have three dogs and walk them every day, which is really good for keeping you fit – and as I do dog agility with them, I do quite a lot of running as part of that.

Trips to the beach are a regular part of Andy's fitness work.

5 Intervals and specifics

RIDERS WHO KNOW their horses well may be content to monitor their
fitness levels by 'feel' and judge progress according to the horse's performance, reactions and recovery. However, some will find this approach
too vague and will prefer a more structured method. This is where
interval training, a system which moved into equestrian sports from
human athletics, can make a huge difference. It was introduced into the
world of horse sports in the 1970s by Jack Le Goff, who was trainer to the
American three-day event team and the basic principle is that the
athlete, whether horse or human, carries out set work periods over a
specific time, with intervals at walk to allow for partial recovery.

It takes time and discipline to set up a suitable work area and learn to
ride at set speeds, but provides a much clearer picture of a horse's ability
to undertake work and recover from it. Interval training can also be the
answer for riders who live in flat parts of the country, such as the East
Anglian fens, where the nearest thing to a slope is a molehill.

Interval training has several advantages. It allows you to make structured,
gradual increases in work but, because the work periods are short, there is
less risk of injury and fatigue. There is also minimal risk of lactic acid
building in the muscles, as any which is produced should be dispersed
during the rest periods. The downside of this method is that some horses
become excited by it because they anticipate what is coming next. This
means that good going on which to carry out the work is essential, and
you also need to make sure that you are in control – which may mean a
temporary change in tack to allow you to work your horse at set speeds.

To start with, you need to mark out one or more areas of 400 m (440
yards) on good going so that you can learn to establish the correct
working speed. The ideal is a proper all-weather gallop, but few riders

Interval training can be carried out on any good going: here, on a peat track in the East Anglian fens.

A heart rate monitor makes life easier and is often used by endurance riders.

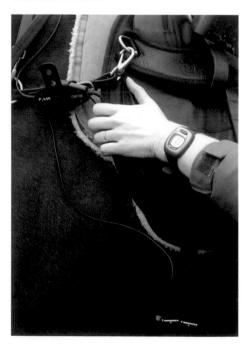

have access to such luxury unless they can get the use of a local race-horse trainer's facilities; most have to be content with the side of a field. It is sometimes suggested that a grass verge can be used, but apart from the fact that this will usually contravene local authority regulations, there will usually be hazards such as small drainage outlets and possibly discarded litter as well as other obvious dangers. If you have enough room, it is better to mark out several 400 m distances on a similar gradient than having to keep using the same one.

You will also need a stopwatch, or at least a watch with a clearly visible second hand, to time yourself over the set distance and for timing your horse's pulse and respiratory rates: this is how you will judge the progress of your work. For event and endurance riders in particular, a heart rate monitor makes life easier since it allows the rider to check the heart rate without dismounting.

Interval training is not designed to be carried out every day, but to be incorporated into the rest of your work. It is usually recommended that it be done every four days and, as a rough guide, you are looking at around six weeks of interval training to reach Pre-novice event fitness, compared with nearer to four months for a three-day event.

Interval technique

Before you start an interval training programme, you should have worked through to the end of stage 3 in the basic fitness work, as outlined in Chapter 4. You also need to establish some base figures and techniques; start by recording your horse's heart rate when you have tacked him up and brought him out ready to work and do this for several days until you have a baseline. It is normal for the heart rate in this situation to be higher than when he is standing at rest, as he will have the stimulus of his surroundings and the anticipation of work.

When you have warmed up your horse, you also need to spend a few minutes establishing the speed and rhythm of the trot you will be working from. With the aid of a stopwatch, ride your 400 m (440 yards) at an active trot, timing how long it takes you. You are aiming to cover the distance at 220 m (240 yards) per minute, which should take 1 minute 49 seconds, so once you have timed yourself you will know whether you need to put more or less activity into the gait. Once you have established what the correct speed feels like, which may take several sessions, you are ready to begin.

For your first session, warm up in walk, then trot for 2 minutes, walk for 3 minutes to allow a partial recovery, then trot for another 2 minutes before stopping and taking the heart and respiration rates. As soon as you have done this, walk for a further 10 minutes, then record the rates again.

The reason you monitor the heart rate and how it increases and falls back to hopefully just above your 'ready to work' base rate is that this allows you to assess your horse's response to work and his recovery from it. As a guideline, approximate heart rates are:

Resting 35–42 beats per minute
Standing ready for work 40–65
Active walk 60–80
Active trot 130–150
Canter 120–170
Gallop 160–200
Maximum racing speed 205–240

When he is fit, has finished work and been through the final rest interval, you can interpret his resulting heart rate through the following guidelines:

100 beats per minute – he is working, but could work a little harder.

120 – a good level to aim at, as it means he has worked hard enough and recovered well.

150 – at this level, you have overdone it for the stage of fitness and need to go back a stage.

200 – a heart rate of 200 beats per minute after the final recovery phase means that there is a significant degree of anaerobic respiration. Unless you are deliberately carrying out anaerobic work, this is too high. If anaerobic work is deliberate and has been done correctly, the horse's heart rate should fall to about 120 within a minute of stopping. Any higher means you have overdone it.

As the idea of interval training is to build up the horse's tolerance to stress, you may find that at first, his heart rate will be higher than 120 beats per minute, though not as high as 150.

The respiration rate should never exceed the heart rate. If it does, stop the session for that day and let the horse recover. When you start your next session, go back a step and make sure that recovery rates are normal.

Over the next few weeks, follow the same method of repeated trot work and walk periods, gradually building up the length of time you trot for and the number of repetitions, until you have reached the stage where you are carrying out three sessions of trotting for 3 minutes and walking for 3 minutes. Trot one more session of 3 minutes, then halt and take the heart and respiration rates. Finally, walk for 10 minutes and take them again.

Once the horse is recovering well from the above routine, increase the duration of the trot periods to 5 minutes but reduce the number of repetitions – so you trot for 5 minutes and rest for 3; trot for 5 minutes and rest for 3; trot for 5, halt and take the heart and respiration rates; walk for 10 minutes and take your readings again.

So far, so good? Then you can now bring canter work into your routine, but first you need to establish the correct speed, as you did with trot. Go back to your 400 m (440 yard) track and aim to ride it in canter at a speed of 350 m (383 yards) per minute, which will take 1 minute, 8 seconds. At the same time, try to estimate what sort of canter you will need to cover the 400 m (440 yards) in 1 minute, as you will be moving up to this in your final sessions.

When introducing canter work to interval training, increase the warm-up period to half an hour in walk and trot. Then canter for 1 minute, 8 seconds; trot gently for 3 minutes; canter for another 1 minute, 8 seconds, then halt and take the heart and respiration readings. Walk for 10 minutes and take them again. When returning to halt, make gradual transitions from canter, through trot and walk.

As with the first trot sessions, you can gradually build up the canter times until the horse is cantering for 3 minutes, trotting for 3 minutes, cantering for 3, then returning to halt whilst you take his readings. This is then followed by the final 10-minute walk period and heart and respiration rate checks.

As his recovery rates improve and become stable, you will feel him finding the work easier. You can then either increase the duration of the canter, or build up to three canter periods. If necessary, you can then move up to the stronger canter you estimated earlier – covering 400 m (440 yards) per minute – starting with two canter periods and building to three when his recovery rates indicate that this is appropriate. When he copes with this and you are happy with his work and his recovery rates, you should be ready to compete in an affiliated Pre-novice horse trials.

To increase fitness beyond this level, for example if you were aiming a horse at a three-day event, you might build up to a total of three 5–6 minute canters. Keep in mind that, as you get to the upper end of the programme, it is important to warm up in walk and trot for 20–30 minutes before starting your timed sessions, and to cool down in the same way at the end of them. As you increase the number and intensity of the canter sessions, increase the time you spend trotting during the cooling down period, ending with 10 minutes of walk. If you are working in hot conditions, and especially if there is a combination of heat and humidity, make sure that you are aware of the latest recommended techniques for cooling down without problems (see Chapter 6).

Points to remember

Interval training sounds like number crunching, but think of it in terms of a basic system that can be adapted to your horse and environment. To gain the maximum benefits from it, you need to be disciplined and methodical and to remember the following:

- If the horse appears distressed rather than acceptably stressed during training, stop and let him recover and if necessary, get him checked out by your vet. Signs of distress include gasping for breath, stumbling and reluctance to move forward. Less extreme warning signs such as the horse changing leg frequently should also be taken seriously. The respiration rate should never exceed the heart rate.

- Conversely, for interval training to be beneficial, you have to raise the heart rate.

- It is vital to measure pulse and respiration rates and not simply to ride set distances in set times. Rates and their recovery after 10 minutes show you the amount of stress the horse has been subjected to and how well he has recovered from it – in other words, how fit he is.

- It is better to build fitness gradually. If monitoring heart and pulse rates shows that the horse is becoming fit quicker than his fitness at the start of the programme led you to expect, play safe and increase the distance covered rather than the speed he is working at. It does no harm to go back a stage, then build up again.

- Never skimp on your warming up and cooling down periods.

The speed test system

The speed test system is another idea that has been adapted for horses from the field of human athletics. Although it is used by some racehorse trainers and event riders, it does not seem to have the wide appeal of interval training. However, as with all methods of fitness training, there may also be riders who are using it in a modified form because experience has taught them that it works – even though they do not put a specific label on it.

Sometimes described as a fitness philosophy, it is a three-phase approach and at the end of each phase the horse is put through a speed test to gauge progress. In general terms, the first phase alone is enough to get many horses to the basic stage of fitness; the second and third phases build on that base and the third phase is probably most applicable to racehorses, event horses at Intermediate and Advanced level and horses taking part in endurance race rides.

Exponents of this system say it builds a higher level of fitness than other training methods without raising levels of stress. It can also be useful for horses who become bored by interval work, as it offers more variety.

Phase 1, which for a mature horse usually covers about three months, is designed to strengthen bones, ligaments and tendons and comprises slow work: two or three weeks of walk only, followed by walk and slow trotting built up to 3 km (1.86 miles) daily of mostly trotting. Canter is then introduced and the horse builds up to doing 10 km (6.2 miles) every third day, most of it at a slow canter. The days in between would be spent on easier work, with the horse having one or two days off out of seven.

To avoid overstressing the horse and to give the body a chance to recover from any unseen damage, the horse is worked in a four-part cycle, each lasting one week. The first week encompasses moderate work, the second hard, the third moderate and the fourth easy. Advocates of this system say that the horse has a chance to recover from any damage done during the hard week before he is asked to work at that level again, whilst more traditional methods allow damage to build up unnoticed until it reaches a certain level.

At the end of this period, the horse is given short gallops of 200–600 m (220–660 yards) and the heart rate is monitored. These gallops are sometimes called 'fartlek', which is Swedish for 'speed play'. In human athletic training, speed is adjusted according to the terrain and how the runner feels – but as a horse can't tell you, monitoring is essential.

Speed play is only carried out once or twice a week and never during the 'easy' period.

Before a horse moves on to phase 2, a speed test is carried out in the form of a moderate (as opposed to racing) gallop over 4 km (2.5 miles) and the heart rate is compared to previous results to check that it is within the required parameters. Satisfactory progression may also be open to the trainer's interpretation and, especially in the case of racehorses, may involve comparison with peer animals in training.

Phase 2 centres on the respiratory system and the muscles, which means increasing the amount of fast work. This is usually carried out twice a week at greater speed, but over shorter distances than those employed during phase 1, though the other days follow a similar pattern. Phase 2 will probably last for about six weeks, when the horse will be put through another speed test.

Phase 3 is based on the work the horse will do in competition and therefore upholds the principle of getting him fit for a particular purpose. Racehorses do a form of interval work at the gallop whilst a Novice event horse would do the same at competition speed.

Blood testing and endoscopy

For most riders doing most jobs, a horse's heart and respiration rates provide good indicators to fitness levels. Blood testing and endoscopy may also be used – routinely in racing and much less frequently in other disciplines – to give additional information or as part of investigation into a problem. For instance, if a horse does not respond to a fitness regime as expected, or his performance and/or response suddenly deteriorates, your vet may suggest one or the other.

Blood testing or 'taking bloods' as many trainers call it, involves analysing the proportions of the various cells in the blood. Samples are always taken when the horse is at rest, as a sample taken after exercise will not give a true picture: the spleen stores blood so that this spare supply can be released when the system is under stress.

Analysing blood can give a huge variety of information, such as the number of red and white cells, the thickness of the blood and enzyme levels. For instance, an enzyme called Gamma GT is a liver enzyme which often increases gradually as a horse's work level increases. If a horse is pushed too far, Gamma GT levels increase suddenly and dramatically, so comparing samples and readings with earlier ones can help show if this is the case. Levels of another enzyme, CPK (creatine phosophokinase) increase when a horse suffers from exertional rhabdomyolysis – commonly known as azoturia or tying-up – so can be measured to help confirmation of a diagnosis.

Endoscopy enables a vet to see what is going on in the horse's respiratory system by inserting a fibre optic flexible tube through one of the nostrils into the respiratory tract. The most sophisticated systems are linked to a video camera, so you can actually see the cleanliness or otherwise of the airways on screen. 'Scoping' is carried out routinely in most racing yards and horses usually accept it with surprising equanimity. It is a standard procedure when investigating suspected cases of RAO and other conditions such as laryngeal hemiplegia, where one side of the larynx is not fully open and the horse's airflow is partly obstructed.

Strength and suppleness

For a horse to perform well and stay sound, he needs to be both strong and supple. The term 'strong' is often applied colloquially to a horse who pulls against the rider's hands, but the strength we are looking to build as part of a fitness programme means the power of the horse's muscles. Some experts believe that strength training is frequently neglected and that as a result, many horses fail to reach their potential – not just through lack of strength, but because they are more prone to muscular and joint injuries.

Some of the best ways to build strength include working across gradients and on hills, with techniques varying according to the horse's maturity and the work he is being aimed at. Gradual uphill slopes are universally beneficial; steep ones can also be useful, but must be approached with care. Walking up a steep hill encourages each hind leg to push independently, which some experts say can help horses who are stronger on one side than the other; walking down such steep slopes on a repetitive basis is sometimes used for horses who are asked to perform rapid accelerations and decelerations, such as polo ponies. However, the horse's muscles are more likely to become sore through downhill work on steep slopes, so thorough warming up and cooling down are essential – or take a leaf out of the endurance riders' books and, if you are doing a form of interval training using steep hills, ride up, dismount and walk down. Cantering up steeper slopes is a good way of developing strength in the hindquarters, especially for jumping.

Working across a not-too-steep gradient can help the horse who has asymmetrical muscle development, provided that you have first taken veterinary advice to make sure that there is no underlying problem that needs to be treated. By positioning the horse so that the weaker leg is uphill, you ask him to flex it more than the stronger one: because this will take more effort, sessions should be kept short. If you want to improve strength through both hind legs, alternate the direction, spending the same amount of time working each way.

Gymnastic polework and jumping is also extremely useful, and not just for showjumpers and eventers: working over poles on the ground and jumping through low grids is beneficial for dressage and endurance horses – see Chapter 9 for suggestions. And just to prove that some of the old horsemen knew what they were doing – even if they did not know the scientific reasons for why their methods worked – modern research suggests that draught work may be another way of building up strength. This involves getting horses to pull weights, starting with very light loads and building up to heavier ones. A century ago, 2-year-olds on the farm would start their education pulling light chain harrows for short periods; as their strength built up and they matured, they would progress to other tasks until they were able to do a full day's work ploughing, drilling or carting.

Suppleness can be defined in many ways, but one way to think of it is the horse's ability to bend and flex in both directions and to use his joints with maximum efficiency without undue effort: conformation can obviously have an effect on how easy a horse finds it to work in balance, but schooling and techniques such as massage and stretching (mentioned in Chapter 10) can improve any horse.

Case history

Fittening notes of an endurance rider

Linda Hams is a dedicated and successful endurance rider who proves that you can get to the top of your sport and at the same time, hold down a demanding job. She has taken three horses from scratch to advanced level in endurance and competes both in the UK and abroad; she has ridden both as an individual and as a member of the British intermediate team.

At the time of writing, Linda rides two pure-bred Arabians, whom she keeps at home. Perfeq Camilla May, or Clover, is a 13-year-old mare who has competed up to and including 160 km (100 miles) ; she came fourth over that distance as an individual in the FEI three-star in Holland. Perfeq Hidden Challenge, or Rowan, is 8 years old and Linda's careful staging of his career resulted in a sixth place in his first race ride.

Linda Hams with Perfeq Hidden Challenge (Rowan).

LINDA HAMS

Fitness philosophy

Getting a horse fit means striking a balance between putting in the work and avoiding unnecessary wear and tear. With Rowan, especially, I'm starting to talk about the quality of the work rather than the quantity.

The old way of training endurance horses used to be to ride them every day of the week, but I've found that scheduling time off into their regime means you get muscle rebuilding in the rest phase and that's made a big difference to my training. You also have to take into account the mental aspect, for both horse and rider.

Feeding

My horses live out all the time, literally 24/7 and come into an outdoor corral with a field shelter when needed. I feed Primero, a fibre and oil based feed; Dodson and Horrell's Build-Up, because it gives a certain amount of necessary starch; Dengie Alfa-Oil, which is alfalfa with an oil coating; soaked sugar beet, linseed oil, vitamin E and salt. When they're competing, they also get electrolytes and five days before a competition they get probiotics which help to retain a balance of the gut flora prior to and during periods of stress.

It's important to keep them hydrated all the time and vital on rides. On the first two circuits of a competition they probably won't want to stop and drink, but the crew offers food and drink on course from circuit three onwards. Food and drink are offered in all the vet gates and we use syringed probiotics and electrolytes at most vet gates. Crewing also consists of cooling the horse via running sloshes so they don't slow us down – the

horses are taught to accept someone running alongside and handing me a plastic container of water, which I can then slosh over the horse.

Schooling and fitness

I start every horse with a month of walking, which is good for them mentally as well as physically – it's all about control. Everyone else's horses will be cantering on the stubble fields and mine will be walking unless I specifically ask them for a different gait. I'll start with five sessions of walk work a week, gradually increasing the time from ½ to 1½ hours; distances will be from 3 to 8 miles and I occasionally put in a small amount of trot because otherwise your backside hurts! Walk work exercises every muscle, but must be done properly. I don't let them just slob around, I go out thinking we're going somewhere. I'm trying to build slow-twitch muscle fibres, not fast-twitch ones.

Even at walk, I choose good surfaces, grass and tracks with a very small amount of work on tarmac. The concussion is minimal but still enough to help achieve bone density. The horses are shod all round; during the endurance season they usually wear pads under the shoes for extra protection against flints but the pads come off in winter to help build up the defences of the soles.

The next stage involves sessions of between 40 minutes to 1½ hours, using trot as a warm-up gait and canter as a fittening one. I don't use trot for fittening because it doesn't build the heart rate up to where you want it. For the first couple of weeks I'll do 5 minutes of canter, not worrying about the speed but keeping an eye on it. I'm more con-cerned about the heart rate – when I'm cantering, I want the heart rate to stay up to 150–180 beats per minute in training. I use a downloadable heart rate monitor all the time when training as well as in competition. What I can't find in Norfolk is any 'five minute hills'; hills which take that time to go from bottom to top, so I'm planning to go to Wales for some training sessions that will give the cardiovascular stress I'm looking for.

Another strategy I've been advised to try is to use a rug on the horse whilst working. This means that although they build up heat, they can't lose it immediately, so you're building healthy stress. It's important to emphasize that this is healthy stress as opposed to distress. You have to do everything possible to make fittening as easy as possible.

I'll gradually build the canter work until the horse can canter for 30 minutes. The canter speed will be faster than I would do in competition and will raise the heart rate to 150–180 beats per minute, whereas in competition it's around 130 beats per minute. In training, you keep the heart rate up because you're looking to build the anaerobic threshold. We aim to stay in aerobic in competition – anaerobic uses glycogen, which tires the horse more quickly.

I find that you have to tailor training methods to individual horses, because they react in different ways. For instance, I don't do regular interval training as such with Rowan because it fizzes up his brain, though I am thinking about putting one interval session a week on the local racing gallops into his schedule. I do interval training much more with Clover, who can take it mentally. Before we moved to Norfolk I had a hill I worked on by cantering up it, then walking down. Here, I use the gallops and also box to Thetford Forest, where there is a long, straight track that you can use for a 10-minute fast canter.

Using a rug can help build 'healthy stress'.

Canter work will be built up until the horse can canter for 30 minutes.

The endurance season beings in March and ends round about the second week in October. Out of season, the horses will do light exercise. They love doing what they do which means they love going for rides – if I give them anything more than a short break when we go on holiday they get bored and would probably start amusing themselves in ways I didn't want them to. They need that endorphin kick and if I didn't give it to them they would find it for themselves. I take them on pleasure rides, which I always feel might not be a pleasure for other people taking part, as Clover is a hugely competitive horse and if she sees another one in front, wants to be in front of him.

Schooling helps build core strength, so is very important and I'm currently looking for someone to work with.

My horses are very lucky and have regular massage sessions from Angie O'Brien, who is a qualified therapist. I even get one myself sometimes! Apart from the fact that the horses enjoy it and it's undoubtedly good for them, it really helps to have a literal 'hands-on' from someone experienced who sees them regularly, but not all the time like I do. Angie is very quick at spotting if a horse feels tight or uncomfortable in a particular area and remedying it.

You have to be very careful with the equipment you use, too. My bridles are synthetic and like everything apart from my saddle come from my husband Steve's business, Performance Equestrian. My saddle is leather and is a Pegaso, which in design is a cross between an endurance and a cavalry model. I use stirrup irons with bushes which have a cushioning effect on knee and ankle joints and never use anything new, either tack or clothes, in competition. Something can start off fine, then cause a tiny rub, which can develop into a major problem by the end of a ride.

Linda's tack and clothing is worn in at home – she never uses anything new in competition.

Rider fitness

My diet and fitness, both physical and mental, is as important as the horses' because if I'm not fit, I can't do them justice. I don't eat meat but I eat fish and I eat lots of pasta and fruit. It's important to keep hydrated and I aim to drink 3 litres of water a day – in fact I drink very little other than water and don't drink tea or coffee.

In competition, I have to make a weight of 75 kg (11 st 11) lb including tack. You have to eat and drink on a competition ride and I rely on currant buns and bananas, plus electrolyte drinks as well as water when necessary.

I use several methods to build my fitness, apart from running and walking with my dog. During last season I ran twice a week, swam once a week and occasionally did some skipping – which is really hard work – to build cardiovascular fitness. With running, I start at 1–1½ miles and build up to 3 miles. Swimming sessions last for 20–30 minutes and I'd do 5 minutes of swimming lengths, followed by 5 minutes of 'running' or 'scissor legs' in the deep end whilst holding on to the sides.

I concentrate on my fitness a lot in the winter, out of the competition season. I do Pilates for core strength, yoga for suppleness and I might do some cycling as well as running, skipping and swimming. I'll probably do about 20 minutes skipping twice a week, so it becomes a form of anaerobic exercise.

The mental approach to my sport is very important and I've had a lot of help from Pete Taylor, a rowing coach. He looks at horse and rider as a team; we set goals and he's really helped me change my attitude. My crew have noticed it when I'm under pressure – now we plan the strategy for each ride so we know exactly who is doing what and when.

6 Fit for all conditions

WHEN YOU ARE getting a horse fit, you obviously want to subject him to as few risks as possible. The word 'risks' is used here deliberately, as subjecting a horse to increased stress – within a safe and acceptable limit – is by definition part of the fittening procedure. As we have already seen, by gradually increasing the amount you ask of him, you should also increase his ability to cope with more demanding work. But as everyone who owns horses knows, there are times when they can seem like an accident on four legs waiting to happen: and whilst no one, hopefully, would be silly enough to work on treacherous going, it can be tempting for riders who have access to perfectly maintained arenas and all-weather canter strips to spend most of their time on these ideal surfaces.

Unfortunately, this throws up three big problems. One is that your going might not be as ideal as you imagine; the second is that your horse will become institutionalized by working within the confines of an arena and become bored and/or be more likely to become over-excited in other environments. The third, very real risk is that a horse who habitually works on level going with the perfect amount of 'give' will become tired and not be able to keep his balance in the real world outside the arena. This tends not to be a problem for endurance horses, who hopefully train over different types of terrain as a major part of preparing for rides, but can catch out showjumpers competing outdoors during the summer season and, in particular, event horses.

Event organizers in all disciplines are nowadays aware of the need to provide good going and, at the top of the tree, events such as Burghley and Badminton go to enormous lengths to prepare and protect the going

A peat track that has been firmed up by the passage of vehicles can provide good going.

on the cross-country course. Measures range from aerating the ground to roping off the take-off and landing points at fences so that spectators walking the course do not wear away the ground cover before the horses get there. However, cross-country is still cross-country and the terrain varies throughout the competition world. As Olympic event rider Jeanette Brakewell reveals in the case history at the end of this chapter, horses still have to cope with ridge and furrow and softer going, particularly at lower levels.

It therefore makes sense to get out and about as much as possible so that your horse gains confidence and isn't put off by the real thing. Basic precautions are essential; protective boots can save a horse from a brushing or overreach injury and if you can't walk the area first to check the going, be cautious and watch out for potential slippery or deep patches. It is also essential to be confident that you can control your horse in the faster gaits before going out to do canter work on unfamiliar ground. If you take your horse hunting, you will have to make your own decision on whether he goes booted or bare-legged: one school of thought says that boots are needed for protection, whilst the other believes that when you are out for long periods, as opposed to a few minutes on a cross-country course, dirt is more likely to get between the boot and the leg and cause rubs.

Shoes versus barefoot

Shoes in themselves are designed to give extra grip as well as reduce wear on the feet, particularly from roadwork and hard ground. As most shoes except for remedial ones are now mass-produced, the concave fullered shoe is standard wear for most riding animals. Concave steel is wider on the foot surface than on the ground surface. This and the fullering – the groove running along the centre of the shoe – helps prevent slipping on traditional tarmac and reduces the suction effect of heavy ground.

Over the past few years, there has been increased interest in the idea of horses going barefoot. This really is a decision that has to be thought through for the individual horse, rather than taking a presumptuous stance and declaring that it works – or doesn't – for all types of horses doing all types of jobs. If a horse has hoof horn of good quality then going without shoes may be feasible or even an advantage in some circumstances, but if you have a horse with poor hoof horn quality and perhaps flat feet (as is the case with many Thoroughbreds), it may prove to be impossible. The same criterion applies to trimming and shoeing methods that are often collectively described under the 'natural balance' label, which aim to reproduce the wear pattern on hooves found in horses in the wild. Whilst they have undoubtedly worked wonders for some horses, anecdotal evidence from farriers and owners suggests that they have not been successful with all. Your best ally is still a good farrier who assesses your horse's foot and limb conformation as a whole and trims and shoes him to achieve good foot balance.

A farrier who takes on a new client should look at the horse standing square from both sides, in front and behind, and see him trotted up in-hand. This will enable him to assess overall conformation, the flight pattern of the hoof and the way the foot lands on the ground. According to the textbooks, a horse should be trotted up every time before he is shod or trimmed, but in practice, most farriers who are familiar with their charges only ask for this to be done if there is a problem, or during the course of remedial work to assess progress.

It also helps if your farrier is familiar with the type of work and/or competing your horse does and has experience of the challenges they offer. Endurance riding in particular is a test of the owner's care and observation and the farrier's skill; it is the only sport other than hunting where a horse is required to work at different gaits over different terrain for several hours at a time. Factors you and your farrier may think about for this and other disciplines include the type of horse and his (and therefore your) safety. The type and build of horse will affect the weight of the shoe; a lightweight 14.2 hh Arab will not cross Exmoor on shoes that would be appropriate for a 14.2 hh Dales pony used for driving.

A skilled farrier can also help minimize risks when working with a young, unbalanced horse or one with less than ideal movement. Sometimes, the two go together: a horse who is still on his forehand is more likely to over-reach and even the best designs of overreach boot can only give so much protection. And if you are eventing or point-to-pointing a horse with a tendency to forge (strike or momentarily stand on the heel of a front shoe with the toe of a hind one, often resulting in a shoe being pulled off and/or the horse tripping), boots that are long enough to minimize the risk of this happening can be a danger in themselves: there have been cases of horses standing on the bottom of a boot and literally tripping themselves up. (As habitual forging or overreaching are usually caused by lack of balance or the horse becoming overtired, both possibilities need to be addressed before competing. However, horses who are particularly short in the back may be predisposed by their conformation to overreach-ing, and even a slight loss of balance or rhythm may cause them to forge.)

In these cases, your farrier may suggest using front shoes with rolled toes, which make for a smoother break-over (the point where the foot leaves the ground). Because it is then easier for the horse to lift his forefeet off the ground, he is less likely to overreach. In the same way, your farrier may also want to leave the horse's hind shoes slightly longer than normal; this gives extra support further up the limb and may also be recommended for a horse with a conformational weakness in a hind leg, such as hocks that are straighter than is ideal.

In recent years there has been an increase both in radical trimming methods and in the number of owners who opt to trim their horses' feet themselves rather than employ a farrier to do the job – unfortunately, the two scenarios often go together. Having said that, there are undoubtedly cases of DIY trimming prompted by a shortage of farriers in a particular area, notably the Highlands and Islands of Scotland. But whether or not you wish your horse to go barefoot, trimming a horse's feet is a skill that cannot be acquired with a DIY internet course. If the correct balance is not maintained, the result will include stress on the limbs, resulting weakness and perhaps lameness; in the case of young horses, incorrect trimming can lead to limb deformity.

At present, only the UK regulates its farriery industry, through the Farriers Registration Council (FRC). Legally, the Farriers Registration Act 1975 regulates and restricts the preparation of a horse's foot to receive a shoe, but simple trimming and rasping is allowed by lay people. However, if in the course of doing this the animal was caused to suffer, the result could be prosecution. The Highlands and Islands of Scotland have been exempted from the 1975 Act, but the FRC's Scottish executive is looking at extending it to include them. At the time of writing, the USA is looking at regulating farriery, but at the moment anyone there can shoe a horse; also an Act is before the German Parliament to bring in something similar to the UK and it looks as if Denmark will follow the same route.

Whilst experts in the UK stress that there are many people capable of trimming feet, all warn that it is not to be taken lightly. As vet Karen Coumbe, author of *First Aid for Horses* (J.A. Allen) points out, good hoof balance is essential and damage can be insidious and devastating. She emphasizes that it takes several years to train a farrier and getting the feet properly balanced is a crucial and difficult part of the work. Vets and welfare organizations such as the International League for the Protection of Horses (which has seen an increase in the number of horses taken into its centres with foot problems), don't want to see the Act amended to make trimming illegal, because they feel this would only make things worse – if law-abiding owners didn't trim and couldn't get a farrier, they would just see more horses with long feet and associated problems. What the ILPH would like to see – and which makes practical sense – is a prescribed foot trimming course, recognized either by the FRC or the veterinary profession and preferably by both.

If you are tempted to go the DIY route by choice rather than necessity, a statement prepared by the FRC in conjunction with the British Equine Veterinary Association may make you think again:

The preparation of a horse's foot to receive a shoe is regulated and restricted by the Farriers Registration Act 1975 primarily to registered farriers. Simple trimming and rasping of horses' feet is allowed by lay persons under the Act to permit maintenance of foals' and other unshod horses' feet.

Where more radical trimming and reshaping of horses' feet is contemplated there is the potential for creating severe lameness. Experience has indicated this is particularly so where such 'therapy' is undertaken by unqualified persons. Horses suffering from significant foot disease such as laminitis should in any case be under the care of a veterinary surgeon. This is to ensure that appropriate treatment is carried out and that any necessary medication is prescribed, the prime object being the welfare of the animal concerned.

Both the practice of radical foot trimming by lay persons resulting in significant lameness, and/or failure to provide veterinary attention under these circumstances, may engender suffering and consequent criminal proceedings under the Protection of Animals Act 1911.

As a result, the undersigned bodies recommend that owners should only carry out minor work on feet of a cosmetic or emergency nature and that any significant trimming should be carried out by a veterinary surgeon or a registered farrier, who will have been properly trained and strictly regulated by a code of conduct.

Safety and studs

Safety often comes down to security and when the going is less than perfect, you will probably think about using studs – another contentious topic! For some disciplines, particularly eventing and showjumping, studs are an essential part of most riders' equipment – but they are only part of the picture and even those who use them as standard emphasize that safety is as important as security. Nor can they work miracles. For instance, small studs might give a dressage horse competing on grass more confidence in his movement, but won't compensate for a horse being on his forehand or incorrectly ridden.

If you want to use studs, the following guidelines will help keep your horse on his feet without compromising safety...his or yours!

- When deciding what sort and size to use, general advice is that pointed studs are for hard going and square ones for soft. Always use the smallest size that will cope adequately with prevailing conditions.

- Opinions vary on whether it's better to use one or two studs in each shoe. However, the favourite approach with top riders is to use two on each hind shoe and one or two on each front shoe, depending on the ground and the horse's way of going.

- Don't use screw-in studs – as opposed to road studs or nails – except on the appropriate going. Screw-in studs should not be used on the road, where they will cause imbalance.

- Don't load and travel horses with studs in. If they kick out, they can damage themselves, their handlers and the vehicle.

- Clean mud and grit from stud holes with a horseshoe nail and plug the cleared holes with cotton wool plugs soaked in hoof oil or WD40. Some people like specially shaped cotton plugs, available from most saddlers.

- Every time you re-fit studs, first clear the thread with a screw tap – sometimes called a T-tap – and then secure studs with a spanner, usually built into the T-tap handle.

Expert approaches

Top event riders use studs as standard in competition, but treat each horse and situation as a separate scenario. For instance, one leading competitor reports that he never uses studs when schooling at home – when he is never going to be under the same pressure as in competition – because he doesn't want his horses to rely on them. In general, when the ground is hard and slippery or if the going is particularly deep he will opt for two small studs on either side of the shoe. On sandy ground, he often finds studs are not needed. Another top rider uses two studs on hind shoes, with a small stud on the inside to minimize the risk of the horse injuring the opposite leg. He prefers to use a single stud on each front shoe, again to minimize the risk of injury.

Showjumping trainer Carol Mailer points out that horses can cause nasty injuries by striking into the girth area with studs. For this reason, she advises her clients to always use a studguard when jumping – even when studs aren't actually fitted – as a horse who picks up well in front can easily bruise himself badly.

Some experts prefer not to use studs at all, because they feel the disadvantages outweigh the benefits. Show producer Lynn Russell is one of them and never uses studs, even on the horses who jump. Her reasoning is that a horse who is going well and in balance shouldn't need them, even to jump a decent working hunter course. She also feels that horses can get to rely on them and if for some reason you forget to put them in, you can find yourself in trouble. Finally – and this is her main objection – she believes that they can be dangerous.

Lynn says that a lot of people don't bother to take them off to put the horse on the lorry for a short while and says she has seen nasty accidents where horses have kicked themselves, people or the lorry. Her method for producing a sure-footed horse is correct schooling and good riding:

A lot of people try to get a horse on the bridle before he's going forward from behind. If he learns to move from behind, using his hocks, he will also learn to carry himself in balance. Leave the front end alone and concentrate on the back end and in time, the horse will come on to the bridle and stay in balance. I've also found that a lot of people ride so they are in front of the horse's movement. If you tip forward, you're encouraging him to go into the ground rather than to move from behind, because the poor horse is trying to balance himself by balancing you.

Robert Oliver, show producer and former Field Master, says he has never used studs even in the hunting field. Like Lynn, he feels that a well-schooled horse, correctly ridden, will stay in balance. 'Also, we don't use boots when hunting because they cause more trouble than they are worth', he says. 'You only need a boot to slip slightly, or for a bit of gravel to find its way underneath, and you've got a nasty rub.'

Endurance riders avoid studs because they ride for long distances and often cover several kinds of terrain on one ride. However, a good farrier may suggest shoeing a horse slightly tighter than usual for competition, particularly in front – in other words, shoeing to the outline of the foot and not beyond, so that the shoes stay secure.

And if you're a top end Western reiner, you'll be looking for the exact opposite to studs. When Sue Painter's international reining stallion

Whata Smoke competes with rider Bob Mayhew, performing movements such as sliding stops, he is fitted with a set of 'slicks'. 'These are thin, extra wide shoes with countersunk nails that allow the slide without putting stress on the limbs', explains Sue. 'Because they have to be razor thin, he always competes in tendon boots and overreach boots.'

Surface issues

Many riders do most of their schooling, both on the flat and over fences, in an arena. Over the last few years a huge variety of high-tech surfaces have become available and many people regard the traditional sand school as out of date. Having said that, there are still many in regular use which give good service, as long as they are properly maintained – and that's the key to all arenas, no matter how they are constructed or what surface is laid down.

The best going of all is, according to most vets and trainers, well-established, well-maintained turf. Yet many riders, especially in the dressage world, have become paranoid about working their horses on anything other than an artificial surface. When international dressage rider and trainer Jennie Loriston-Clarke ran Catherston Stud as a top competition centre, she was amused by the horrified rider who, when told that the warm-up areas were on grass, protested that his horse only ever went on a 'surface'. What he did not realize was that the grass in question was mature, well-maintained, level pasture that had been down for years and provided the kind of going that arena manufacturers say they strive to imitate!

Grass gallops at two epicentres of the racing world, Newmarket and Lambourn, have seen generations of racehorses thrive. Flat trainers say that horses at Newmarket need more work, both slow and fast, than at other centres to build them up and keep them fit but that the turf of Newmarket Heath takes far less out of a galloping horse than moorland or springy downland.

Lambourn horses have the advantage of on-the-spot hill work. In the hilly parts of Berkshire, reported Tim Fitzgeorge-Parker in the classic *Training the Racehorse* (J.A. Allen 1993) a horse is working as soon as he leaves the yard. Fitzgeorge-Parker found that hills were equally good for jumpers when they came in from grass and said that some, like Hungerford Hill, which gives a long climb out of Lambourn village, was good for the 'slow cantering of bad-legged horses being prepared for hurdling and chasing'. What will surprise many of today's riders is his declaration that 'the tarmac surface should not deter the trainer of such animals from cantering. A rough, hard surface does far more harm to legs'.

Few of us today would canter on the road, at least not deliberately! But there are also different views on whether periods of trotting on the road should be encouraged because this helps 'harden' the legs, or be avoided because it causes unwanted concussion. It is an individual choice, but top competition horse vet Andy Bathe makes the point that if the road surface is level and not slippery, it probably causes less jarring than does uneven ground. It goes without saying that all trot work should be balanced – a hurried or irregular trot is asking for trouble.

The renowned gallops at Lambourn downs were traditionally opened only in the hardest summers. They are covered by downland turf, described by Tim Fitzgeorge-Parker as 'grass of similar consistency to that found above some seaside cliffs where you can burrow with your finger eight inches down through the closely knit mat before you come to soil. You could work six horses on White Horse Hill full stretch upsides and never hear them coming...' Many of today's event riders and endurance competitors use local trainers' gallops as part of their horses' fitness programmes. It has to be said that more than a few dressage horses would probably benefit, both physically and mentally, from the same opportunity.

Risks are not associated only with fast work. Every racehorse trainer knows that pulling up sharply or turning suddenly can injure tendons and ligaments, but the rest of us sometimes forget this. Turning sharply in a jump-off when your horse isn't schooled sufficiently to stay in balance, or asking a horse to perform 10-m canter circles or canter pirouettes before he is strong enough and capable enough to do so can ruin more than your competition plans. The surface you school on can add enormously to the effort your horse expends even to perform the simplest manoeuvres (deep, dry sand, for example) or, alternatively, makes it easier for him to learn to carry himself and stay in balance.

Research is being carried out in the UK into the use of various surfaces, using both racehorses and dressage horses as the models. At the time of writing, only preliminary findings from one study have been published and these are not necessarily relevant to areas outside racing. However, the study offers interesting food for thought.

The study was carried out to try to find out the reasons for distal limb fractures (fractures below the level of the radius or tibia) in racehorses; this is the most common cause of fatalities on UK racecourses. Results showed that horses doing no gallop work during training and those in their first year of racing were at a significantly increased risk of distal limb fractures on the racecourse. The case horses were also more likely to have been trained on sand gallops, defined as gallops described by the trainers as being primarily composed of sand.

Sand surfaces can vary, but safe footing on a beach is an environment that horses enjoy.

That does not mean that sand can be condemned as a training surface, particularly as few horses are either worked or galloped on it as 2-year-olds. However, it does mean that in the future, we may know more about how best and on what surface to carry out certain types of work. Other studies in Germany and the UK may offer information on the sort of impact different surfaces impose on horses' limbs when schooling and jumping.

And if all this makes you long for that mature, well-maintained turf, perhaps the best news is that turf reinforcement is the hottest buzzword in surfaces. Methods range from using plastic mesh or blocks in the soil, to 'top dressing' with fibre. For more information, see *All-weather Surfaces for Horses* by Ray Lodge and Susan Shanks (J. A. Allen).

Working with the weather

You don't need to be a scientist or an expert on global warming to appreciate that climatic conditions have changed across the world. From the point of view of working horses, the most important change is the increase in periods of heat and humidity. This first hit the headlines in a big way when Atlanta was announced as the venue for the 1996 Olympic Games; as leading researcher Dr David Marlin explains, the Barcelona Games in 1992 caused problems and some of the horses finished the cross-country phase of the three-day event very distressed, but the climate was hot and dry compared to the double whammy of a hot and humid Atlanta.

We don't know exactly how hot horses became in Barcelona, says Dr Marlin, because the only thermometers available at the time were designed for humans and as such, only registered up to 42 °C. Horses are able to tolerate much higher – and lower – temperatures than people, but many who finished the cross-country course were off the scale. Problems came about not just because of the heat, but because of the increase in demands placed on horses and riders: as riders became better at training, courses needed to present greater challenges to separate them out.

When Atlanta was announced as the next venue, a three-way partnership started between the Federation Equestre Internationale (FEI), the Animal Health Trust (AHT) and the International League for the Protection of Horses (ILPH). At the time, these Games were highly controversial and one school of thought held that they should be cancelled or moved elsewhere. But as Dr Marlin points out, moving them was never really an option and the only alternative would have been for the horse sports to have been pulled out – which, with hindsight, would have been a retrograde move both in terms of horse sports, horse welfare and research. Before Barcelona, there were only about twenty-five scientific publications relating to horses and heat; between Barcelona and

Atlanta and leading on to the 2008 Olympics in Bejing (Hong Kong for the equestrian disciplines) there has been an enormous amount of research that will benefit everyone who rides, whether at riding club or international level.

The first thing we have learned, says Dr Marlin, is how to transport horses better. If you take a horse into any unfriendly environment and he is already tired, dehydrated and disorientated before he gets there, you are not giving him the best chance of recovery. Researchers learned from exercising horses in carefully controlled conditions of heat and humidity in staged surroundings at the AHT how they would respond, what warning signs to look out for, what was a reasonable workload if it was hot and humid and whether all horses could acclimatize to heat and humidity.

One fact that emerged was that if you are working a horse in conditions of combined heat and humidity, the demands on him may be 20 per cent greater than in cooler ones. Researchers also learned more about thermal stress – for instance, they now know that a fit Thoroughbred who is on the lean side, fully clipped and on the right diet, given electrolytes when necessary, does not have problems when acclimatized in hot, humid conditions. Acclimatization is a key element, whatever you are aiming your horse at: at a basic level, it may be tempting and seem kinder to work your horse in the cool of the early morning, but if you're intending to take part in competitive disciplines where you have to go and pull out all the stops in much hotter and possibly also more humid conditions, you need to get your horse used to working in them and learn to manage him so he is not distressed.

Olympic lessons

Lessons from the Olympics can help all of us take the heat out of competition. The golden rule is that we must make sure that horses are hydrated, as opposed to dehydrated, which may mean changing both your management routine and your preconceptions. One simple management technique that can make a huge difference is to take a horse's temperature daily, as this will give you a baseline to work from. If you take it again before transporting or working him – or if you have the slightest suspicion that he is not quite as bright as usual – you can spot problems right at the beginning. As Dr Marlin points out, if you stress a horse when, for instance, he is starting to get a virus, you may also double the time it takes to get him back to normal.

Dehydration can be a huge problem and can even prove fatal. Studies of human athletes have shown that even small losses of fluid can lead to loss of co-ordination, reduced awareness and other ill effects and the same applies to horses. This doesn't mean that you should avoid making your horse sweat, but that you should make sure he is able to replace what he loses.

As we saw in Chapter 3, when a horse sweats, he loses both fluids and vital electrolytes, which need to be replaced. Horses sweat in a number of situations – not only when they are working for long periods, or working hard for relatively short periods, but if they are upset or excited and often (for a combination of reasons) when they are being transported. Unfit horses will lose more sweat when doing the same work as a fit horse and nervous or excited horses may sweat more than relaxed ones in the same situations – all of which goes to show that getting a horse physically and mentally fit has wide-ranging benefits.

Sweating is the major natural method of thermoregulation.

Sweating is basically good for the horse in that it helps to keep him cool, but excessive or prolonged periods of sweating will cause dehydration. It is a potential problem that we must always be aware of, as horses may sweat more than normal if, for instance, there is a very hot day in spring when previously the weather has been cool – in other words, when they are not acclimatized. Dr Marlin says there has been evidence that, each spring, a number of National Hunt horses collapse from heat stress after finishing a race. Movement of air over the horse's body helps keep him cool whilst racing and the high heart rate keeps blood pumping round the body from the muscles and through the skin. But as the horse pulls up, airflow is reduced and the heart rate and blood flow slow down – and at this point, body temperature may reach a maximum and signs of heat stroke may appear.

During tests in controlled, simulated hot and dry and hot and humid conditions, horses became unsteady during a minute's rest during the simulated phase C section of an event, but as soon as they started walking, they settled and became more comfortable. The lesson is to avoid coming to a sudden stop and keeping your horse standing when you have finished working, especially at the end of a competition. Instead you should cool him with water, using the wash and walk technique, alternating short periods of washing with short periods of walking.

Cooling with water is a big help to a horse. It used to be thought that putting cold water on to horses caused muscle damage and possibly tying up, but research has shown otherwise. Iced water is sometimes used in extreme conditions, but this is probably needed only when the horse's rectal temperature is more than 41.5 °C. Don't just concentrate on cooling the front end and forget about the back end; to be effective you need to cool the whole body.

Think about your warming up methods on a hot day, too. Physiologically, the horse will not need as long a warm-up, though obviously you also need to take his mental state into account – however, don't be tempted to overwork. Older horses are often more susceptible than younger ones to heat, though some horses, like some people, just find it more difficult to work when it's hot.

If you're competing or working a horse hard in hot conditions, think about clipping him to keep him more comfortable. This may be advisable even if you think you're not working him hard – a heavier type of horse may have a dense coat even in summer and as such, will often be more comfortable if clipped. Just as important, don't do anything to impede the natural sweating process; at one time many riders smothered their event horses' legs and even their chests with grease in the belief that this would help them slide over fences, but as horses cannot sweat through grease, it is counter-productive.

Taking a horse to water

The old saying that you can take a horse to water but you can't make him drink has a despairing ring of truth for owners worried about horses who won't drink away from home. However, there are ways round it; for a start, some horses will drink if the bucket is held for them, whilst others are tempted if the water container in the stable is emptied and refilled with a fresh supply. In hot weather, some horses find water which has warmed up unpalatable, but will drink if it is replaced by a fresh, cold source. My Connemara pony always drinks when his water container is filled from a hose – perhaps the equivalent of preferring his tipple on draught! Other techniques which can be successful in persuading the reluctant drinker include:

- If you are competing or travelling to ride away from home, take some containers with your own water. Water from different areas tastes different; if you are away for a long period and can't take enough, mix home water with local supplies, starting with a high ratio of home to away water and gradually altering the balance.

- Borrow techniques from endurance riders and add peppermint cordial or apple juice to the water. This will often tempt horses who can't be persuaded to take plain water. Another method is to offer very sloppy sugar beet, but this should be made up with one of the sugar beet products formulated to need only a few minutes soaking, so there is no risk of it turning sour in hot weather.

- If your horse is reluctant to drink in his stable, try re-siting his water bucket or container. When a team at the AHT studied behaviour in a group of horses, they found that some would not drink when the bucket was near a door or window, perhaps because they felt vulnerable with their heads down near an opening: as Dr Marlin points out, a frightened horse will run to the back of his stable, away from the door. If horses drink outside, they will lift their heads at a sudden movement or unusual noise, so if your horse feels safe, he may be more inclined to drink. Similarly, put water containers higher in the stable rather than at ground level. The study group showed that some horses preferred drinking from a bucket in a wall clip rather than one on the ground.

● Some horses drink more readily in their stables if their water is provided in mangers which hang on the door. This way, they can drink and still watch everything that is going on outside. The mangers obviously need to be re-filled regularly and it is sensible to provide another source of water inside the stable.

Case history

Fitness pointers from a top event rider

Jeanette Brakewell is not just one of Britain's most successful eventers – she must also be one of the most hardworking. She is consistently successful with a wide range of horses throughout the grades; in 2005 she scored wins and placings on twenty-three horses, from Novice to Advanced. However, she is best known for her partnership with the brilliant 16 hh, Irish Thoroughbred Over To You, a competitor at the top level into his late teens and whom she partnered on a record-breaking seven consecutive British eventing squads. Their most notable wins include team silver medals at both the Sydney and Athens Olympic Games and two team gold medals at World Equestrian Games.

Jeanette Brakewell and Over To You.

JEANETTE BRAKEWELL

Fitness philosophy

Although the cross-country format has changed, I still lean towards the Thoroughbred as the perfect event horse. The cross-country course itself is still the same length and the horses have got to be just as fit. I don't mind a touch of something else in the breeding, though – and in any case, a lot of modern Warmbloods are mostly Thoroughbred. It's more the stamp and type of horse that I pay attention to: he can't be too heavy and his wind has to be good.

Temperament and attitude are really important. A horse has obviously got to have ability, but he's also got to have a trainable temperament and not be too hot-headed. Certainly when you get to top level you've got to know that you can go into the arena and the horse will let you ride him; you don't want to be on a time bomb that's waiting to explode.

I'm open-minded about whether I ride a mare or a gelding. If you get a good mare, they're very good. They might be quirky in other respects – for instance, I've got one at the moment who is grumpy in the stable, but as soon as you're riding her she's willing to do everything for you. An event horse has got to be willing and forward going.

It's easier to work with a horse who is kind in the stable, but I wouldn't necessarily be put off by behaviour such as crib-biting. The proviso is that it doesn't affect their soundness or their ability to hold weight. Similarly, with conformation there are some technical faults I don't mind and some I don't like. I don't mind if a horse is a bit over at the knee because that takes the pressure off the tendons, but I don't like one who is back at the knee, because that puts the pressure on. Good feet are important and I don't like a horse to be too long in the cannon bone or pastern.

Some people won't look at a horse with a curb, but as long as the hind leg conformation is reasonable, it doesn't bother me. Over to You has got a curb and it's never affected him – and he's been competing at top level since he was 10. And although the dressage phase is important, I wouldn't go for a horse with really flashy paces, because that puts more pressure on the legs. I want a horse to have good enough paces, without being flashy.

Feeding

Our horses get as much time in the field as possible, according to the ground conditions. If they go out regularly, they are less likely to get silly in the field, but if they are turned out infrequently, they are more likely to get excited – which is often when accidents happen. With an older horse such as Over To You, it definitely helps to prevent them stiffening up.

Our feeding programme is based on Spillers Horse Feeds and every diet is based on a scoop of Horse and Pony Nuts, with Happy Days chaff and soaked sugar beet. Any horse who needs a bit more weight on gets Spillers Showing and Conditioning Mix and if a horse needs more energy in the build-up to a three-day event I feed High Digestible Fibre Slow Release Sports Cubes.

We feed Eurobale big bale haylage rather than hay, because the quality is consistent and you don't have to soak haylage. With the number of horses we have on the yard, we get through a bale a day. They get two hard feeds a day, because I feel that as long as they've always got roughage, the digestive system is always working.

When horses are stabled we use Belvoir Equizorb bedding, which is easy to manage, gives a good base and provides a healthy environment.

Schooling and fitness

I build up basic fitness the traditional way; it's the way I was taught and it's always worked for me. I start by doing six weeks roadwork, just walking for the first three to four weeks and then adding a bit of trot. Once the fitness base is established, schooling, canter work and hill work – when possible – are added. When I was based in Norfolk, which is not exactly hilly, I used a local trainer's gallops which incorporated a small hill and, in Leicestershire, we were been able to use Paul Webber's training gallops. In Staffordshire, there is lots of off-road riding.

When you're working out a fitness plan for a three-day horse, you have to start from your competition date and work backwards, so the horse hopefully peaks at the right time. Once a horse has reached peak fitness, it's easier to work back to it when they've had a break. With an older horse, such as Over To You, time in the field is important, because he's moving around most of the time as he grazes. When he's not in work, he also goes on the horse walker every day.

I don't need to do interval training now, but have used it previously and would build up to three lots of 7-minute canters with a 4-minute gap in between. I think people used to gallop horses too much: I'm sure I did. That's when you risk horses getting tired and injuring themselves as a result.

Different people have different views about the surfaces they work on, but I feel that whilst you would never want to risk a horse on bad going, you can't have perfect ground all the time when you're competing, so your horses have to get used to different surfaces. If they didn't, their legs wouldn't adjust to what you get in a normal British Eventing competition, especially at lower level. Events are pretty good most of the time, but you still get ridge and furrow and some fields that are a bit softer than others – and horses have got to be able to cope with that. Similarly, when you go cross-country schooling the ground is sometimes slightly slippery and again, without taking undue risks, the horses have to learn to stand on their own feet.

I like to keep the horses' work routines varied, a mixture of schooling, hacking, jumping and different competitions. They always get the day off after a competition and they're trotted up first thing to make sure they're sound. If there are no problems, they either go out in the field or on the walker. You have to know what your horses' legs are like normally and check them regularly – my girls will tack up the horses for me, but they never put the front boots on. They leave them off so that I can check the horses' legs and then put them on myself.

Jeanette Brakewell and Over To You competing at Burghley.

Saddle fitting is important but on a big yard you can't have a saddle for every horse, though Over To You has his own, because he isn't shaped like any of the other horses! I use Amerigo saddles with wool flocking and usually one saddle will fit three or four horses of the same width and shape. The saddle has got to fit the horse; you can make slight adjustments with pads and so on but there's only so much you can do.

Rider fitness

Riding and working keep me fit. In the summer, when I'm busy, I often find I don't have time to eat enough and the weight stays off. I have to remind myself to drink enough water, though, because if you get dehydrated you're not riding properly or safely.

7 Competing for fitness

MOST RIDERS AIM TO get their horses fit to compete in a particular discipline. As such, competing at appropriate levels in target and complementary disciplines can be used as a way of building and assessing fitness as well as an end in itself and is a good way of building sport-specific fitness. Any horse who has successfully completed stages 3 or 4 of the basic fitness regime suggested in Chapter 4 should be ready to perform a dressage test or two in competition surroundings, to complete a lower level endurance ride or take part in a showjumping competition.

The level of competition must, of course, be tailored to the horse's experience as well as to his fitness and the principle that you should be working at home a level ahead of your competition outings can be a sensible one: for instance, if you are jumping 1 m (3 ft 3 in) courses at home, competing over 0.75 m (2 ft 6 in) ones will allow for the extra difficulty imposed by strange venues, travelling, working-in with other horses and so on.

With the young or inexperienced horse, who has even more 'sensory overload' to cope with, it is worth taking him on an outing or two just to ride round, especially if he has never actually competed before. He will find travelling and all the sights and sounds so much to take in that he will probably be tired by the acclimatization; next time out, he will know what to expect and you can fairly ask him to take part in a showing class, a Preliminary dressage test or a small showjumping competition.

In-hand showing can be a curse or a blessing, depending on how sensibly it is approached. Young horses who have been overfed to produce show ring 'condition' and dragged out every weekend rarely seem to go on to performance careers and, because the extra weight puts so much strain on their joints, they stand less chance of staying sound. Fortunately, the

Pleasure rides with optional fences are another way of assessing and building fitness.

message does seem to be getting across – though there are still notable exceptions – and the potential in-hand and ridden classes for young sports horses promote soundness and athleticism, with judges penalizing overweight animals.

Your horse's behaviour and performance at and after a competition will help you decide how well your fitness programme is going and whether he is actually ready to compete, or needs more acclimatizing. You need enough 'fuel in the tank' for him to perform the task without being overtired by it, so you should not have to spend more than 20–30 minutes warming up once you have done your initial walking.

Unfortunately, young and inexperienced horses sometimes find the competition environment so exciting that it is impossible to get straight on and walk round. In this case, the best option is to find an area where you will not interfere with other competitors and lunge the horse for a very short period. Ten minutes will often be enough to take the edge off and you need to be aware that if you have to work him hard to settle him, any effort after that will be correspondingly harder.

Horses who come off the lorry or trailer with their eyes on stalks are not always the easiest to handle, especially if you are trying to remove travelling gear and put on protective boots – essential for warming up, as an excited horse is more likely to knock himself. If you think he is going to be a handful, the best strategy is to travel him in bandages over padding rather than boots. Tape over the fastenings for security, ensuring that the tape is no tighter than the bandage, and you will then be able to ride or lunge your horse in his travelling bandages until he has settled enough for you to remove them and, if necessary, replace them with competition boots.

Getting there

Travelling your horse may not, at first sight, seem to be part of a fitness regime. However, it is a form of stress in itself and can have such a profound effect on his well-being that you should never take it for granted – though hopefully, he will! It is important to minimize travel stress, which can affect horses both physically and mentally, by taking every precaution in the way you kit out your horse for a journey, load him and travel him and also in the attention that is paid to the environment in your lorry or trailer.

Travelling gear

The main purpose of travelling gear is to protect a horse from knocks and scrapes whilst travelling, but you also need to make sure that he maintains a comfortable body temperature. A constant flow of air through the vehicle is important to keep his respiratory system healthy but, against that, you do not want him either to get cramp in his muscles because he cannot move out of the way of cold draughts, or become overheated.

The horse's legs are vulnerable to injury and should always be protected, even on short journeys. The only exceptions are foals and inexperienced youngstock – though it is a good idea to get yearlings upwards used to wearing travelling gear at home so they accept the unfamiliar feeling. Whether you choose travelling boots or bandages over padding comes down to individual preference; modern designs of boot are quick and easy to put on and are shaped to cover knees and hocks, but if a horse kicks or stamps, they are not usually as stable as bandages. It only takes a boot to slip slightly for an irritated horse to become even more irritated, and if it slips enough to frighten him, you've really got problems.

Bandages take longer to put on and remove, but can be fastened with tape as suggested earlier in this chapter and worn for working-in. The more you practise putting them on, the quicker and more efficient you will become, especially if you apply bandage and padding in one step. Open a short length of bandage, place it below the top edge of the pad and then wrap both round the leg, continuing the bandage down; this holds the pad securely without the risk of creases and is much easier than the textbook method of wrapping a layer of padding round the leg and holding it whilst you bandage in place. If you want to provide padding over the knees and hocks, use bandage pads that are shaped accordingly. Knee and hock boots may do the job, but have to be fastened so tightly at the top to prevent them slipping that this in itself may cause problems.

The padding should provide enough protection for the coronet band and heels, but if your horse tends to tread on himself or has a knack of pulling off shoes in transit, travel him in overreach boots. If necessary, you can fit these all round.

Tail bandages help prevent horses rubbing the tops of their tails, but with big horses, or those who tend to lean back, you can give more protection by applying a tail bandage in the usual way, then putting a piece of thick foam rubber cut to size on top of the dock and putting a second bandage over this. Padded poll guards which fasten to the headcollar can also be useful for big horses or those who tend to throw up their heads; head-collars should be leather rather than nylon, as the latter may not break in time in an emergency and can cause severe injury. Lead-ropes should be secured to breakable twine. Pressure or 'controller' headcollars are some-times useful for re-educating horses who are difficult to load, but should never be used to tie a horse up.

Some horses have a knack of pulling off front shoes whilst travelling, usually because they are trying to find their balance and tread on the heels of the front ones with the toes of the back ones. Considerate driving will help a horse to stay balanced, but you can minimize the risks of lost shoes – or worse, overreach injuries – by fitting overreach boots. Similarly, a horse who treads on the coronet of one hind foot with the other foot can be protected by using overreach boots behind. You can buy coronet boots expressly for this purpose, but overreach boots are usually cheaper and do the job as well.

Rugs should be chosen according to weather conditions and those in your vehicle. You need to keep the horsebox or trailer well ventilated, but at the same time to protect the horse from draughts. Since a horse can't move out the way of draughts in transit he can arrive with cold and stiff muscles so, even in hot weather, it is a good idea to use a thin cooler or cotton sheet. In colder conditions, lightweight knitted thermal rugs are ideal; these are also excellent for putting over a horse in cool weather after he has worked hard and perhaps sweated slightly, as they keep the muscles warm and wick away moisture.

Although you don't want to transport your horse's whole wardrobe, it's essential to take spare rugs, even on hot, dry days. Apart from the fact that weather conditions can change, a tired horse feels the cold more. Magnetic rugs have become enormously popular with many owners (see Chapter 10) and some vets and physiotherapists recommend them for use before and after exercise – but because they are said to increase blood flow, it is usually not a good idea to use them when actually transporting a horse, as he may end up sweating.

Large or wide horses, or those who try to lean against a wall or partition, sometimes bang or scrape their hips. If you have this problem, check that there isn't an obvious cause; for instance, driver error or a horse partitioned into too small a space. Some horses have definite ideas on the position in which they feel comfortable travelling and will be far happier in a layout with herringbone stalls, where they can stand on the diagonal, or rear-facing ones. Although most will travel facing forwards without problems, some find it harder to balance in this position – though inevitably there are horses who prefer it! There are rugs available now with padded sections on the hips to offer extra protection.

If you use a trailer, you will have to travel your horses facing forwards unless it is one of the few models designed specifically to take horses facing backwards. Never travel a horse backwards in a standard trailer, as it is not designed to take weight distributed in this way. If you carry a single horse in a trailer with a partition, put him in the bay behind the driver to counter the effect of road camber; if you are travelling two horses, put the larger one on the driver's side for the same reason. It is dangerous (and illegal in the UK) to travel a forward-facing horse without a breast bar.

Occasionally, horses are said to be happy travelling in a horsebox but not in a trailer. Although there may well be some cases where this is true, an experienced and considerate driver and handler can usually find the cause and hopefully put it right. A common scenario is someone driving a sophisticated tow vehicle which gives a comfortable ride and assuming that the trailer affords the same comfort to its occupants at speed: it doesn't. You may also find that a horse who seems restless travelling alone with a partition will be relaxed if you take the partition out and let him choose his own travelling position: this will usually be on or towards the diagonal. A single horse in a two-horse trailer needs full-width breast and breech bars; don't be tempted to use a single horse trailer if you find such a rarity, because they are unstable.

If you have a horse who is difficult to load, you may find that he is easier to get into a well-designed trailer than a horsebox, as trailers have low, gradually sloping ramps. Sometimes you see luxurious horseboxes with ramps so steep that horses have almost to jump up them: no wonder they aren't always happy at the idea! If you have problems loading into a lorry, or are teaching a young horse to load, it's often better to use a trailer as a stepping stone to teach him to walk on and off quietly.

Specialized loading and travelling techniques are outside the remit of this book, but as you will probably need to transport your horse during fitness preparation as well as when you are ready to compete (and always without undue stress), transporting is an area that needs careful consideration. For sources of in-depth information, see the Appendix at the end of this book.

Healthy travelling

Do think about the effect of the horse's travelling environment on his respiratory system and try to apply the same principles as to stabling: good ventilation with minimum dust and mould spores. If you feel that your horse will be happier with a forage net, feed haylage or soaked hay, preferably the former; soaking hay for the outward journey may be simple, but coming back could pose a problem. Don't fasten spare supplies to the rear ramp, or it will be a magnet for engine fumes and dirt thrown up off the road and you will present your horse with a polluted haynet on the return journey.

Long journeys demand special planning and management. Jackie Potts, head groom to leading event rider William Fox-Pitt, likes to offer wet hay in mangers in the horsebox rather than haynets. This means the horse isn't putting his head up, which helps with drainage through the sinuses. Every 4 hours, she stops at a safe, suitable place and takes the horses off the box for 20 minutes to let them walk around and pick grass. Again, putting their heads down helps the drainage.

If you can't take your horse off the lorry, stop for a break and untie him – obviously staying with him and keeping hold of the lead-rope. Feeding carrots from the floor will again help drainage through the sinuses and, because of their high water content, they help keep him hydrated.

Every sensible horse owner has first aid kits at home for humans and horses, but you should have separate ones for travelling that can be carried in the horsebox or tow car. Vet Karen Coumbe suggests the following items to make up a travelling first aid kit for horses; although this might sound obvious, remember to replace used items:

- A digital thermometer. Old fashioned mercury ones are no good in this situation, as they can overheat.

- A roll of cotton wool for cleaning wounds and to use as padding under bandages. Moist antiseptic wipes are also useful.

- Moist wound gel to protect and cleanse a wound. The generic name is hydrogel but brand names include Vetalintex and Derma Gel.

- A good antiseptic such as Hibiscrub or Pevadine.

- Scissors with curved ends.

- As many bandages and dressings as you have room for, but especially:

  – Non-stick dressings in a variety of sizes to go over wounds. Brand names include Melonin or Rondopad.

  – Stretchy conforming bandages such as Vetrap or cheaper gauze ones that need to be taped. The former are easier to use in less than ideal situations, which is usually what you're faced with!

- Surgical, insulating or duct tape to hold bandages that need to be taped (or poultices) in place. If you need to poultice a foot, you'll need duct tape for durability and strength.

- Animalintex to use as a poultice.

- Cool bandages or pads designed to be soaked in water and used as a first aid measure for inflammation.

A question of attitude

If you are using a competition as part of your fitness build-up, to give your horse experience of coping with new surroundings or to assess whether your training at home is paying dividends in the 'real world', it's important to remember that those are your priorities. It's always nice to come home with a rosette, but it's far better to go for a slow clear in a jump-off if your horse isn't ready to be pushed – or even to withdraw from a second round if he is starting to feel tired – or to miss out fences on a hunter trial course if you feel him flagging. We can all say that of course we would do that anyway, but at the same time, it can be really tempting to go for it when your blood is up, especially if you are competitive by nature.

If you can't envisage yourself competing for experience rather than going out to win, then find different ways of adding variety to your horse's work until you are sure he is ready. For instance, a non-competitive sponsored or pleasure ride with optional jumps may make you less tempted to push too hard. Similarly, many training centres and competition venues run showjumping evenings, particularly in the winter, when you can take a horse round a course designed by an official course builder – so you know the distances will be correct. These sessions often start with fences at a low height suitable for novice horses and/or riders and heights are raised at regular intervals. The idea is to encourage and give experience, so if you have a problem at, say, a particular combination you will find that the organizers will lower and adapt it to help you solve your problem.

Showjumping and dressage clinics with experienced trainers who can spot when a horse is starting to flag are also good options – and give you the benefit of an experienced outside eye who can spot weaknesses in your horse's way of going and suggest strategies to help. Don't discount these even if you have regular lessons, as a session with a different, well-recommended trainer can sometimes spark new ideas. He or she might suggest the same overall strategies as your regular teacher, but a different way of explaining something can often make a difference.

Case history

Keeping native ponies busy and happy

Julia Woods has backed, schooled, produced and competed a huge number of native ponies, both her own and for other breeders and owners. She is particularly well known in the Connemara pony world, where she has partnered top performance ponies such as Croxton Portia and Elaphine Murphy, but has also been involved with New Forest, Dales, Fell, Highland and Welsh Section C and D ponies. Julia is also a member of several judging panels and has judged at the Horse of the Year Show.

She is renowned for her ability to understand the mentality of native ponies – which as anyone who owns one will appreciate, is very different from that of a Thoroughbred or Warmblood – and for getting the best out of them. All the ponies and part-breds in her care lead varied lifestyles and whilst they may excel in the show ring, they also enjoy plenty of hacking and jumping; many excel in mountain and moorland working hunter pony classes and more than hold their own in unaffiliated one-day events.

Julia Woods with her home-bred Mystic Moonlight, still in work at the age of 24.

Until recently, Julia achieved her many successes without the use of a manège, which riders in many other disciplines would find unthinkable. She says that even though she now has one available, it gets very little use! Even so, her ponies can and do perform well in dressage up to Novice level.

JULIA WOODS

Fitness philosophy

I've always thought of the ponies I have as performance ponies, who show as part of their lifestyles, rather than show ponies. This means they have varied workloads, with hacking and jumping and hopefully aren't fat. You also have to take into account the pony mentality: you can't school them every day in an arena like you can some horses, because they just switch off.

To get them fit in the first place you have to build up gradually. Because mine live out all or most of the time, they get semi-fit just mooching about all day – I've had people ask me how you get horses fit from grass, but I don't understand how they get racehorses fit when they're standing in a stable 23 hours out of 24!

If a pony is backed but hasn't been in work when he comes I start with lungeing, but as soon as I can, I get them hacking out. I have had some 3- and 4-year-olds in for breaking who were basically just not strong enough to start any sort of work regime and when that happens, the best thing is to back them, walk them round so they get used to a rider and then send them home for six months. When they come back, they're usually a bit stronger and you can go on from there.

Sometimes, they come in as 3-year-olds like gawky teenagers. It's often a good idea to sit on them, because they don't have the energy to buck you off, but you can't overwork them because it causes problems mentally.

Feeding

Native ponies need a high-fibre diet and until recently I've had fields of old, established pasture. It wasn't fertilized but it was rested and droppings

The animals in Julia's care live out most of the time.

were picked up regularly – I spent my life picking up piles! At my new yard the grass hasn't been down for as long and is a richer mix, so I'll probably have to strip graze part of the time. Because the fields are smaller, I'll also be picking up piles even more often.

I feed hay rather than haylage to any who are in at night, because I like to be able to give a big enough net to last all night and I couldn't do that with haylage. The hay doesn't have a high protein level but it is clean. It must be better for the digestive system if they aren't going for long periods without eating – I think that could be one reason why some people have problems with colic. All horses need to be fed in a way that's close to nature, but it seems to be even more important with natives. I'm sure a lot of laminitis is caused by nutritional imbalance.

Whether or not they get hard feed depends on

Native ponies need a high-fibre diet. Julia feeds clean but low-protein hay rather than haylage.

the work they are doing and their type. For instance, one Connemara x Thoroughbred on the yard is competing in Pre-novice horse trials and is out in the day and stabled at night; he gets Baileys Topline conditioning cubes for extra fuel and because he isn't as much of a good doer as a pure-bred Connemara would be.

I don't feed supplements as a matter of course, only if they are needed for a specific purpose, but I do put salt licks out.

Schooling and fitness

Everyone says that to get the most out of a horse, you have to think like one. That's true – but I think that people fall into two categories, those who think like horses and those who think like ponies! You can't take native ponies into a school every day and drill them, because they'll just switch off. You have to give them variety; if you do the same hack every day they'll find something to look at or spook at just for the fun of it.

I do a lot of my schooling out hacking and expect them to work properly all the time, with a free walk on a long rein every now and then to let them stretch. They've got to use their back ends, not just amble along. Depending on how fit they are at a particular stage, they would get more or less frequent rest periods on a long rein.

When I trot along a track, I ask myself what it would look like if the pony was in the ring or in the dressage arena and aim to get the picture I want. If they don't know any different, they're not going to question it. They know that this is the contact, this is my leg, this is the rhythm I want them to take. I'm careful to get good transitions and if I want to move away from a car or an obstacle, I will specifically ask the pony to leg-yield or turn, not just move over any old how.

Julia does much of her schooling out hacking.

I'm always amazed when I take clinics just how many people will let their ponies do things they don't want them to. They say, 'Oh, he leans on the right rein' and my attitude is: well, why do you let him instead of showing him that you don't want him to? Natives in particular are so clever that the only way you can tell them you don't like something is not to let them do it! They will soon latch on to the fact that, for instance, you'll hold them up round left hand bends and the only way they'll understand is if you make them use their inside hind leg rather than using your hand as a support.

Although I don't do formal interval training as such, we do go off and have a mixture of walk, trot and canter. Sometimes if we're going cross-country, I will give them a 'blow' beforehand.

It's really important to know your ponies as individuals, because you have to push some of the naturally lazier ones. If you didn't know them, you'd think they weren't fit enough to do the job.

My ponies usually do mountain and moorland working hunter pony classes, so they do hunter trials and one-day events as part of their preparation and to keep them interested – they usually love it. My reasoning is that when they're happy tackling all the sorts of fences they meet cross-country, they won't be fazed by anything they are likely to meet in a workers' class. You sometimes see ponies competing and get the impression that they've only ever jumped coloured fences.

Because I'm usually busy looking after other people's animals, my own ponies are usually worked every other day once they're at the right level – and because they're out all or most of the time, they're on the move and hopefully keeping their fitness much better than if they were stabled for long periods.

Trotting up hills builds strength and fitness: Julia on David Bartholomew's part-bred Connemara, Coogan Sedge.

We're lucky here in that we do have hills. At my previous yard, there were fields on a hill and I deliberately put one pony on the hill as a young-ster to build up his back end. Trotting up a hill is a good way to get them to work. I don't trot on the roads a lot and certainly don't hammer them, but I think a little trot work like this can benefit them as long as you're sensible about it. I've never had any problems caused by it and I've never had one who can't cope with firmer ground.

People now get problems with natives that we never used to see and I think one reason is that some riders get fixated about having to work on 'a surface'. I run a small show on lovely old pasture, offering Prelim. dressage competitions and showjumping up to 76 cm (2 ft 6 in) – and the amount of people who decide they can't do it because it's on grass and not on a surface is quite surprising. I think that's quite a widespread attitude, though, except perhaps with eventers.

Rider fitness

Mucking out, yard work, riding and lots of walking seems to keep me fit enough, though I don't think I'm perhaps quite as fit as I was when I was going up and down the hill fields all the time. Come the summer, I'm riding three a day; I don't smoke, don't drink very much and fortu-nately come from reasonably slim stock!

8 Groundwork

ALTHOUGH MOST FITTENING work will be done under saddle, lungeing, long-reining and systems such as that developed by Linda Tellington-Jones (see TTEAM Work, this chapter) can also play a valuable part if done correctly. In situations such as parents trying to keep small ponies fit for children to ride, particularly in the winter, when school commitments and shorter days mean that riding is often only possible during weekends and holidays, they are essential skills. As vets know all too well, ponies who have been out in the field for long periods, who are suddenly brought into work for school holidays and asked to do more than they are ready for, can be prone to all sorts of problems. In particular, a pony who has been out on good grass and is then faced with a busy time of hacks, shows and so on during the summer holidays is vulnerable to laminitis associated with concussion.

Groundwork activities can also be mainstays for the working owner battling against a shortage of daylight hours – and even if you have plenty of time to ride, they are valuable additions to your horse's regime. Not only do they add variety, they enable you to watch your horse moving and working without the weight of a rider on his back and you can learn a lot from watching the way he moves and carries himself. For instance, if he tilts his head to one side when you are riding him, but not when being lunged in a cavesson, common sense should tell you to get his mouth and teeth – and your riding – checked. Never ignore small warning signs like this, as a horse who carries himself even slightly off balance is going to put extra strain on another part of his body; this is why hind limb problems often become back problems.

Lungeing can be hard work for a horse, so it must always be done on good going. It can also be boring – just think of the phrase 'going round in circles' – so it should be done in moderation. With a young or unfit horse, start with a 10-minute session and build up gradually. Even with a fit horse, you should not need to exceed 20 minutes or, at most, half an hour at a time. Whatever the overall lungeing period, it should always be divided into equal times on both reins and you should not lunge every day; two or three times a week will be beneficial but not boring.

Long-reining with two reins can be carried out in straight lines or on a circle. Circle work is obviously as repetitive as lungeing, so the same attention must be paid to the boredom factor and to the number and length of the sessions. Long-reining in the form of driving – with the handler behind the horse and working him in a straight line – can be done outside an arena, for instance round fields and tracks, but whether or not you long-rein a horse on the road depends on whether your circumstances make it a safe option. It certainly isn't something that could be advised if you are working alone with a young horse, one who is unreliable in traffic, or on busy roads.

Safety first

No matter how reliable your horse, safety precautions are vital. Always wear a hard hat and gloves when lungeing or long-reining, even if your horse lunges like the proverbial clockwork mouse. Learn from my mistake: several years ago I forgot to take my gloves into the schooling area and decided that, as the horse I was lungeing was experienced and reliable, I would do without. That was the day a local farmer decided to test his bird scarer; my horse took off, the lunge rein whipped through my hand and bent my finger to the side and I have a permanent lump on it to remind me of my folly.

If you are long-reining outside the school – even if you are using fields and tracks – wear a fluorescent, reflective tabard so that you can be seen from a long way off by walkers, cyclists, drivers and riders. For safety's sake, it is advisable to position yourself slightly to one side of the horse, swapping regularly from one side to the other, rather than walking directly behind him. Not only does this make you less vulnerable if he shoots backwards and kicks out; you are visible to others approaching from either direction and also have a better chance of stopping a horse who decides to take off. If you are directly behind him, you will become a reluctant water skier, but if you are slightly to one side, you are in a much better position to turn and then stop him.

To protect your horse, always fit boots all round when lungeing or long-reining; ones with fluorescent, reflective bands add extra protection when riding or long-reining on the roads. When you are long-reining in straight lines (driving) you may feel safer if the reins are passed through stirrups or the side rings of a roller, as explained later in the section on long-reining techniques.

Lungeing equipment and techniques

If you are not experienced at lungeing, or have only lunged horses who know what it's all about and now want to teach a young horse, it's important to think through the equipment you use and lungeing techniques. It's possible to lunge by fastening the lunge rein to the back ring of a well-designed, fairly snug-fitting headcollar – and one school of thought says that this is actually better, as it works from the control point from which the horse is used to being led. Advocates of this system say that the conventional system of fastening the lunge rein to the centre front of a lunge cavesson noseband may also inhibit the horse's desire to go forward. However, the general view is that it's best to start off with a standard lunge cavesson, designed to stay in place without slipping and with a reinforced noseband incorporating three rings for a choice of attachment positions for the lunge rein.

At first – and in some cases, throughout – you will be lungeing the horse from the cavesson, not directly from the bit. If, later on, you want to use side reins or other lungeing aids that attach to the bit, you will need to use a bridle, minus noseband, under the cavesson. The bridle should be fitted so that the cheekpieces of the lunge cavesson go under the cheek-pieces of the bridle, thus minimzsing unwanted contact on the bit. Some trainers prefer to use a Wels cavesson, which fits lower on the nose and, when used with a bit, is fastened like a drop noseband. This gives more control but is also potentially more severe.

Lunge reins are made in many types of material, but the best and most comfortable to use are cotton webbing, either plain or with hand stops similar to those used on Continental web reins. Most lunge reins have a hand loop at the end, but whilst this should be large enough to allow your hand to slip in and out, you should never be tempted to wrap the rein round your hand; if the horse takes off, so will you, with potentially dire consequences.

The best way of holding a lunge line so that you have maximum control and also maximum sensitivity is to hold the rein in your inside hand and the spare loops in your outside one; so when you are lungeing on the left rein, the rein will be in your left hand and the loops and lunge whip in your right hand. On the right rein, the rein will be in your right hand and the loops and lunge whip in your left.

The commonest way of teaching a horse to lunge seems to be with a helper who – according to the method – either leads the horse round on the circle, walking on his outside, or stands between the trainer and the horse and signals with the lunge whip. Adherents of the first method find that it helps the horse to understand the principles of going forward and on a circle; however the second is not recommended because, unless commands are perfectly synchronized, the result is usually a confused horse.

It is often simpler for one person to teach the horse, so long as it is done logically and in safe surroundings. As you can't expect a young horse to understand that you want him to go to the end of a lunge rein and walk and trot round in circles, start by leading him round your school or fenced off lungeing area with the lunge rein fastened to the centre ring of the cavesson. It is easier and safer to start on the right rein, so that you are between him and the fence: easier, because most horses are accustomed to being led from the left (even though we should all make an effort to lead from both sides) and safer, because if he spooks at something round or outside the arena, he is more likely to jump away from you rather than on top of you.

Using the voice commands you intend to use when lungeing, you should quickly be able to teach him to walk on and halt on command. Your tone of voice is crucial, as commands for upward transitions should be upbeat and encouraging and those for downward ones, slower and soothing. Some people like to use the word 'halt' when they want the horse to stand, but good old-fashioned 'whoa' is more drawn out and soothing. When he is confident on the right rein, do the same on the left. The next stage is to teach him to trot in-hand, although if he has been shown in-hand he should already be confident at this. If he does not know what to do, you may need to carry a schooling whip and tap him gently on the side as you ask for trot; be prepared for him to shoot forward the first time and go with him, or you will be telling him to go forward and punishing him when he obeys. When teaching a horse to trot in-hand, it's best to start off leading him from the nearside, alongside an arena fence or other barrier to encourage him to stay straight and not swing his quarters to the outside.

Once he is responding to voice commands, you can go on to the next stage, which is a cross between leading and lungeing. Get him used to the lunge whip by holding it close to him and gently stroking it over his body, then walk a large circle – on the left rein, this time, as most horses find it easier – standing about 3 m away from him. This means you will walk a slightly smaller circle than he does and you can introduce the idea of forming a triangle with the horse as the base and the lunge rein and whip as the two sides. Keep the whip pointing towards his quarters but with the end resting on the ground at first; as he gains confidence you can raise it as necessary. If he understands and responds to the voice commands, all well and good; if he doesn't, you can step closer to make your signals clearer. Just make sure that you are far enough away to be out of the danger zone if he kicks out.

Some horses get the idea and work happily on both reins right from the start, but others find it more difficult to work on the right rein. This may be for underlying physiological reasons, or because the horse is habitually led and handled from the nearside and therefore more accustomed to bending to the left, or both. If this happens, go back to leading from the offside and gradually increase the distance between you and him. When he walks and halts confidently on both reins, introduce the idea of trot. Again, you will move on a slightly smaller circle than him.

Your body position and the way you hold the whip have a big influence on the horse. If you think of your 'neutral' position being as if a perpendicular line from you to the horse would meet him halfway along his body, with the whip pointing towards his quarters, you can encourage him to slow down or go forward to a slower gait or to halt by moving so you are slightly ahead of him. Similarly, moving so you are slightly behind him will encourage him to go forward. If he tries to cut in on the circle, look directly at him and step towards him, shortening the lunge rein very slightly – but without pulling in his head and forehand – whilst you point the lunge whip at his shoulder.

Lungeing gives you a good opportunity to assess and, if necessary, improve your horse's responses and way of going. His walk should be forward but not hurried and hopefully he will overtrack – if you watch his footprints, the print of the hind foot should come in front of that of the forefoot. The trot should be forward and balanced and you are looking for him to track up; the print of the hind foot should come up to that of the forefoot. Cantering on the lunge can be difficult for a young horse unless he is naturally balanced, and if it is asked for too early, or on too small a circle, it can put strain on the hock joints. Cantering on the lunge should be kept to a minimum and should not be attempted until a horse can stay in balance and rhythm in trot on a 20-m circle. Prior to that, if a horse goes forward into canter of his own accord he should be asked to return calmly to trot.

If you want to improve the canter of a physically mature horse, short periods of canter on the lunge can help; some trainers believe that this is even more effective when the horse is lunged with a Pessoa lungeing system (see next section.)

Lungeing from the bit

Although horses should be introduced to lungeing using a cavesson, there are times when you will want to use a bit, either to attach training aids such as side reins or for more control. In a perfect world, control would not be an issue, but in the real one – if, for instance, you are working with a hooligan who has learned to tank off to the end of the lunge rein and keep going – extra measures may be called for. If your young horse has to learn to wear and accept a bit as well as learning to lunge, introduce a bit first and let him merely wear it whilst you lunge from a cavesson. Once lungeing is established, you can introduce side reins and so on.

There are three main methods of attaching a lunge rein to the bit. The first is simply to clip it to the inside ring. This gives a definite, direct contact and can be successful with a trainer who has good 'feel' and knows how to influence the horse with body language and whip posit-ion, but in less skilled hands it can lead to too much inside bend of the head and neck and the horse being put off balance. If you use this method, it's best to use a full cheek or eggbutt snaffle to keep it central in the horse's mouth; if you particularly want to use a loose-ring snaffle, fit rubber bitguards to prevent the risk of the bit being pulled through the horse's mouth.

The second method is to pass the lunge line through the inside bit ring and clip it to the outside one, changing it over when you change the rein: so when you are lungeing on the left rein, the lunge rein will pass through the inside, left ring and clip to the outside, right one, and when working on the right rein, it will pass through the new inside, right ring and clip to the new outside, left ring. With this method, you are less likely to get too much inside bend.

The third method is the 'hooligan special', in which the lunge rein passes through the inside ring, up the face and over the poll and clips to the outside one. This can have a powerful action and when pressure is put on the lunge rein, either by horse or trainer, it raises the bit in the mouth rather like the action of a gag snaffle. It is not a method you would want to use as standard, but desperate times can sometimes call for desperate measures!

Lungeing over fences

Lungeing over poles on the ground and over fences can be a good way of adding variety to your horse's work, especially for riders who simply do not want to jump themselves. It also enables you to increase the demands made upon the horse without adding the complication of a rider's weight.

It is recommended that, when jumping on the lunge, the horse should always be lunged from a cavesson, not from the bit, so that there is no danger of him getting jerked in the mouth. When jump stands are used, a 'sliding pole' should be incorporated so that the lunge rein cannot get caught on them; this is an ordinary jump pole positioned so that one end balances on the top of the wing and the other drops to the ground at the side.

Whilst most people can lunge over ground-poles, you need to be quick and agile to lunge over fences – so if in doubt, don't. If you have never lunged over fences, it is best to get help from an instructor who knows how to and can help you to do it properly.

Training aids

There are many training aids, old and new, designed to improve the horse's way of going on the lunge – and as many opinions on whether they are good, bad or indifferent. Some can also be used when the horse is ridden but, for our purposes, the following are discussed purely in the context of lungeing on the flat (not over fences.) As with any training aids, all should be fitted loosely until the horse accepts their 'feel' and if necessary, shortened gradually. It is always best to warm up without any form of training aid.

Side reins

Side reins are often thought of as standard lungeing equipment, but they are training aids just as much as any other piece of equipment. They are designed to encourage the horse to accept and work into a contact and will in themselves give more control. They should never be used on a horse with a tendency to rear, as if he goes up and overbalances the consequences can be fatal; only last year, I know of a potentially top-class horse who reared, went over backwards and broke his neck when wearing correctly fitted side reins. Some trainers prefer plain side reins and others like to use ones with rubber or elastic inserts, because they feel these have a slight amount of 'give'. The choice is yours, though a horse who tends to lean may do so even more on reins with inserts and will often carry himself better with plain ones.

If the horse has not worn them before, try attaching them to the side rings on the lunge cavesson to start with. Occasionally, a horse will find this irritating and will be happier if they are attached to the bit rings from the beginning. Fasten them to the roller or the girth straps so that they cannot slip, at a height level with the horse's mouth when he is standing in a natural, relaxed manner. Some trainer like to fit them loosely to start with, as they believe that their only influence is then through their own weight. However, if the side reins are so loose that they flap around, this can result in small jerks on the horse's mouth. Aim to achieve the slightest of contacts when the horse stands with his nose just in front of the vertical and as he gets used to and accepts them, you can shorten them gradually – don't be in too much of a hurry to shorten them and remember that the idea is to encourage him to work forward into a contact, not to pull his head in.

There is another type of side rein called Lauffer reins or Vienna reins, which allow more lateral flexion and can work well with horses who hold themselves behind the contact or try to lean on the bit when fitted with ordinary side reins. Each rein passes through the bit rings, from inside to outside so as not to have a pinching action, and has an adjustable fastening at each end. They fasten to the side rings on a roller and the height of the adjustment depends on the horse's stage of training and way of going. In most cases, it is best to fasten one end to the lower side ring (not the ring underneath the belly) and the other to the centre side ring. If you are working an advanced horse and looking for more collection, you may prefer to fasten one end near the top of the roller and the other to the centre side ring.

The Chambon

This is a 'classical' training aid, but though it has a classical history, it can still be misused! It can have a real value, though, in encouraging a horse to stretch his neck and back and to use his abdominal muscles. It is excellent for persuading horses who have been forced into a false, 'scrunched up' outline through incorrect riding to lengthen, as well as for improving the way of going of horses who have a build-up of muscle underneath the neck. If a horse is truly ewe-necked because of his skeletal conformation, all lungeing and riding equipment – including the Chambon – should be used with care and you have to accept that he will never be able to achieve the posture of a horse with correct conformation. However, most horses appear to be ewe-necked because incorrect work has built up muscle on the underside of the neck and, when worked correctly, they will lose this and build up muscle in the correct place. I have seen the Chambon used to great effect on Arab horses who had previously been shown in-hand and encouraged (or forced) to take an unnatural stance far beyond that of their normal high head carriage.

The Chambon comprises a pad which buckles to the bridle headpiece at the poll and has a small ring at each end to take the running cords or straps from the second, separate piece. Make sure you choose one which is shaped correctly, as unless the headpiece has a slight curve, it may put pressure on the base of the horse's ears and defeat the object.

 This second piece fastens at the girth, like a martingale, and splits into two cords or rolled leather straps, each with a small clip at the end. The cords pass through the rings on the poll pad, down each side of the horse's face and clip to the bit rings. The Chambon works through a combination of poll pressure and bit action – if the horse raises his head too high, the bit is lifted slightly in the horse's mouth and the pad exerts pressure on the poll. Most horses accept it readily, but with a horse who has not been introduced to the idea of poll pressure, it's sensible to fasten the clips directly to the rings on the poll pad first time round.

Only use it for 5–10 minutes to start with, because the horse will be using unaccustomed muscles. As with any training aid or form of exercise, if he starts to ache, he will become tense and defeat the whole object of the exercise – apart from it being unfair to subject a horse to such discomfort.

The bungee rein

The elastic schooling rein or bungee rein is a simplistic version of the Chambon; probably less effective, it nevertheless has its uses. It is nothing more than a strong elastic cord with a small amount of give that goes over the poll and down the sides of the face, where it is passed through the bit rings and can be fastened either to the girth, going between the front legs, or at the sides to girth straps or roller rings.

The bungee rein applies pressure on the poll when the horse raises his head too high, but because of the give inherent in its construction, few horses resent it.

The Lungie Bungie

Developed by event rider Clayton Fredericks and Libbys Tack, this can be used for lungeing or riding. It offers similar benefits to side reins, but does not restrict the horse's lateral flexion and many horses work well in it. An adjustable, slightly elasticated rein passes through a ring on a connector strap fastened to the bit and is fastened to the roller or saddle D-rings on each side.

The Pessoa lungeing system

At first glance, this looks as if you are literally tying a horse up in knots – but it's much simpler to fit than it looks and even simpler to use. It has its critics, as do all training aids, but I have seen it used successfully by

The Lungie Bungie does not restrict lateral flexion.

BELOW The Pessoa lungeing system is designed to help build muscle in the right places.

enthusiasts in several different disciplines and in particular, by showing specialist Lynn Russell, to encourage horses to work more from behind and to put their hind legs further underneath, thus developing a better canter.

Developed by international showjumper Nelson Pessoa, it can be used in four positions, according to the horse's development and stage of training. The first, or low, position is designed to encourage the horse to stretch and work from behind; once this has been established, the middle position is said to improve muscle development and engagement of the hocks. The high position approximates to an 'on the bit' ridden position – though you should not be tempted to go straight to this adjustment without working through the lower ones – and aims to improve the balance of the canter. The fourth or so-called 'dressage position' will only be suitable for a small number of advanced horses and trainers.

Long-reining

Many people are put off the idea of long-reining because they think it is too complicated – but probably the most complicated thing about it is the fact that it can be referred to by several different names. So to try to keep things clear, in our context the phrase long-reining means using two lunge (long) reins to enable you to start, stop, steer and use an inside and outside rein, just as you do when riding. Long-reining on a circle and lungeing with two reins mean exactly the same thing. Similarly, driving a horse or long-reining on the straight/on a straight line are interchangeable terms.

Long-reining is a really underrated activity which used to be part of every horse's education and in some yards, still is. It can be used to help build up muscles, improve acceptance of the bit and even – if you are really skilled – to teach advanced movements such as half-pass, all without the burden of a rider's weight. If you are a parent trying to get or keep fit a pony who is too small to be ridden by adults, long-reining is the answer.

Most animals take to it easily, but because the reins touch the horse's sides and back legs, they must be introduced carefully, in the stable. Attach one lunge rein at a time and, with a helper standing at the horse's head, gradually drape and flick it over the neck, back and sides, until the horse accepts it calmly. Occasionally, a horse will object to the reins touching the backs of his hind legs and the best way to desensitize him is to make a lightweight 'breeching strap' and fasten this to a roller. Let him wear this whilst he is in the stable with plenty of hay to eat and he will soon get used to it touching him as he moves about.

Even if your horse is an older, experienced animal, start off in a safe, enclosed area. With a young horse who is being long-reined as part of his early education – a good way of helping to build up his strength and suppleness – you may want to start by attaching the reins to the side rings on a cavesson, then passing them through the bit rings to the cavesson rings so that you get mostly nose pressure but with a little contact on the mouth, until you are ready to attach them directly to the bit rings.

Many people long-rein successfully in whatever snaffle bit their horse is ridden in, but a lot of experienced trainers prefer to use a mullen mouth (unjointed) bit to give more control. Don't get blasé, even with a horse who is reliable under saddle – a pair of shod hind hooves can do a lot of damage if a horse bucks or kicks out, so make sure you are out of reach.

Long-reining with two reins on a circle makes it easier to maintain the correct bend, as you have an inside and an outside rein. Whether or not you pass the reins through the rings on a roller or a pair of shortened stirrups (which should be prevented from flapping about by fastening a spare stirrup leather through each stirrup iron and under the belly), is down to personal choice. A good rule of thumb is to do this when you are long-reining on a straight line, but to let the lunge lines hang free when you are long-reining on a circle. If, when working on a circle you pass the outside rein through a stirrup or roller ring, as some trainers recommend, you have to stop, unclip it and clip up your new outside rein every time you change the rein. The height at which the reins run through stirrups or roller rings affects their action on the bit; if they are too low, there is the potential for too much leverage. When long-reining in the traditional English method, the reins should run along the horse's sides more or less parallel with the ground.

The Feeline

The Feeline, developed by classical rider and trainer Claire Lilley, makes lungeing with two reins simple and effective. Each end of the Feeline has a small, static clip and a larger, sliding one. To lunge on the right rein, you stand on the nearside with the Feeline coiled in your right hand and fasten the static clip to the nearside bit ring and the sliding one to a ring midway down a roller. Laying the coiled end over the horse's back, you then move to the offside, take the Feeline over the horse's back; holding it in your left hand, you reverse the clip positions and fasten the second static clip to the roller ring and the second sliding clip to the bit ring.

Most people find this much easier to manage than traditional double reins when working on a circle, because you hold a rein in each hand exactly as when you are riding – so you can feel the horse's reactions in the same way and can ask for flexion with the inside rein whilst you control speed with the outside one. Claire advises that, at first, you should keep the outside rein of the Feeline over the horse's back as you work him, but as you both become confident, you can bring it down around his hind-quarters so it rests just above the hocks and maintain just enough con-tact to keep it in that position.

The Feeline makes it easy to lunge with two reins.

Making it interesting

Groundwork doesn't have to be boring. You can long-rein your horse over and around poles on the ground, teach him to move laterally and – if you have a safe environment – take him round fields, tracks and even quiet roads. It is an excellent way of starting walk work and for adults to build and maintain a base fitness in small ponies: as a bonus, you will find that your own fitness improves! If you're energetic, you can add periods of controlled trot when long- reining in straight lines, but introduce this in a safe environment, with caution. Most ponies will accept it, but occasionally a pony will feel that he is being chased and will react accordingly.

Loose-schooling over fences

Loose-schooling in an enclosed area or a round pen is advocated by some trainers as a good way of getting horses to work freely, especially over fences, but – and this is purely a personal view – it can also create problems. Because you have little or sometimes no control over the horse's speed, you can end up with a situation where he goes into the schooling area and never goes slower than a canter. I know of one sensitive horse who was loose-schooled regularly and decided that when you went in an arena, you cantered, even if your rider wanted to trot. It took many months of patient schooling out of an enclosed area before he learned to relax and to go from walk to trot when asked, rather than walk to canter.

At one time, many trainers used jumping lanes: oval tracks with fences built across them. A horse would be put in one end and encouraged to find his own way down the lane, jumping the obstacles without hindrance as he came to them. Many horses loved them, because they were not under pressure. Loose-schooling over fences in an arena inevitably means one or two people using lunge whips to guide the horse, and unless it is done by someone experienced and athletic, it can degenerate into chasing a horse into a fence.

TTEAM work

The Tellington Touch Equine Awareness Method, or TTEAM, was developed in the 1970s by Canadian horsewoman Linda Tellington-Jones and has many devotees throughout the world. Ground exercises are designed to increase the horse's awareness and improve balance and co-ordination whilst a system of circular touches/massage called the Tellington Ttouch is said to activate cellular function. Certainly both approaches can be used to great effect by someone experienced in the technique, such as leading UK exponent Sarah Fisher, and there is a variety of books, videos and DVDs as well as courses available for those interested in exploring them.

Some owners, perhaps particularly in the UK, are put off by the names applied to different touches and to the leading positions used for ground-work. But if you can grit your teeth and get beyond the idea of performing the Clouded Leopard or Lick of the Cow's tongue touches, or using the Dolphin Flickering Through the Waves or the Journey of the Homing Pigeon leading positions, you could reap the benefit. The founder of the systems uses a leading system incorporating a chain across the horse's nose and a rigid white schooling whip – white so that the horse associates it with specific signals during the groundwork – referred to as a wand.

The groundwork exercises are another way of adding variety to your horse's work and encouraging him to think about what he is doing. For instance, the Star is a variation on working over raised trotting poles under saddle, as explained in the next chapter. Four 3.7 m (12 ft) poles are spaced in a fan position, resting about 15 cm (6 in) from the ground on one side, with the ends of the poles touching, and spread out at the other. The handler walks through the star on the higher side, staying two poles ahead of the horse, and as he becomes confident with the exercise he can be asked to go deeper into the Star so that he is lifting his limbs higher. As with all exercises, it must be carried out equally on both reins.

See the Appendix at the end of this book for information on how to find out more about TTEAM and TTOUCH.

Case history

Handling and fitness pointers for newly backed youngsters

Kate Jerram specializes in producing all types of show horses, especially hunters and working hunters. She competes and wins at top level and in recent years has taken coveted titles such as Hunter of the Year at the Horse of the Year Show; she has also produced numerous champion show hacks and riding horses and currently has several top working hunters in her yard. Kate also has wide experience in eventing and helped her father, Mike, train point-to-pointers and hunter chasers.

She is particularly talented at backing and educating young horses and is renowned for being able to get animals who have gone wrong somewhere along the line – usually because they have been misunderstood or ridden incorrectly – to work happily again. All her horses lead varied lives and Kate will often compete them in dressage and, in the case of the working hunters, in indoor showjumping competitions through the winter to give them an all-round education and get them used to different environments. For instance, one of her rides, the Queen's lightweight hunter, March Past, has won dressage competitions at Novice level.

Kate Jerram with one
of her charges.

KATE JERRAM

All of Kate's horses get an all-round education, whatever their main job.

Fitness philosophy

When people send me young horses to back they sometimes ask if I want them to be lunged for a month before they come. The answer is always no, because there's nothing worse than trying to back a half-fit horse who's already got bored from being sent round in circles. I'd far rather have them straight from the field because then you can make sure that they enjoy their work right from the start and you can tell just how much they are ready for at each stage, both physically and mentally.

You want them to be looking to you for help, not looking to see how they can get out of doing something. Keeping them right in their minds is as important as getting them fit physically and

when I go to a horse's stable I want him to prick his ears up and think, 'Oh good, it's her, now I'm going to enjoy myself', not 'Oh no, it's her again.' They have to be happy and kept stimulated, but in the right way.

You have to think about every detail and be aware of how they are reacting to their new environment. We're lucky in that our yard is several small groups of boxes within an overall set-up; some areas are quiet, whilst in others they can see things going on all the time. Some boxes have windows at the front and back so they can see what's happening on the yard from one window and watch horses being worked in the school out the back – some horses love this but some find it too exciting, so you have to match the horse with the location he prefers.

Feeding

The last thing you want is a young horse on rocket fuel, but you also have to make sure they have enough energy. It doesn't matter if they are a bit tired after working and in fact that's inevitable, but you don't want them to be exhausted. We use a lot of Allen and Page Calm and Condition feed, with Baileys Topline cubes for those who need a bit more weight. Good hay is vital and any bales that show signs of being less than top quality would be rejected. Some are fed soaked hay, but because we have really good forage we find that many are fine with dry; our boxes are well ventilated and we have shavings beds that are kept clean.

Kate's mother, Jill, is in charge of feeding: young horses need enough energy for work, but not rocket fuel.

We don't feed supplements as a matter of course, but some things are useful for certain horses. Nupafeed, a magnesium-based liquid, helps keep some horses calm in stressful situations and I like to use Newmarket Joint Formula, which was formulated by Ian Wright, a leading orthopaedic vet, to help maintain joint health and flexibility. For any horses who have a tendency to weak feet, I'll suggest their owners use Newmarket Hoof Supplement, which was also formulated by Ian and which we've found to be very effective. Another thing I like to do is to add a handful of dried nettles a day to some of the horses' feeds. It's a traditional thing that the old grooms used to do and it seems to bring out the dapples on greys and chestnuts.

Schooling and fitness

Most people like to have their horses backed as 3-year-olds because it makes more financial sense, but with my own horses, I've sometimes started them off as 2-year-olds. Obviously when you work with 2-year-olds you have to take their mentality and stage of maturity into account and be very careful not to overdo it. Two-year-olds tend to look to you for help much more: when they get a year older, they are bigger and stronger and can perhaps be a bit more bolshy.

One thing I never do is have 2-year-olds going round in circles, because their joints can't take it. We long-rein them and back them with a light rider, then get them hacking out – they'll usually be hacking out a week after they've been sat on for the first time. The long-reining has taught them to stop and steer without a rider's weight and they learn to go round the farm tracks, so it's no big step to riding out with another horse. The breakers always go out in company and they always want

Kate riding out: she believes that young horses need to be kept interested, not constantly drilled.

to go where the others do, so you don't have problems with them not wanting to go out.

I like to get on with things quite quickly, but that's because I have people I can trust and we can keep the young horses interested and enjoying what they're doing without asking them to do things they can't cope with. It's a case of taking small steps at a time. When they come to be broken, I like to have them for a month to six weeks – you can't get a horse going properly in a shorter time without rushing things and I won't do that.

They do something every day so they don't get bored and I like the breakers to work seven days a week. They're only working for short periods and if they work well, they finish: I don't like to drill them. It's important that they don't get bored, but that they're wondering what they're going to do next and enjoying it.

There are always two of us working with a breaker and I always like to work with the same person, so you know how to work together. It's important that the person on the ground is strong and very aware: you need to be able to look at the horse and be aware of the way he's reacting and moving. You definitely don't want someone on the ground who is slow thinking.

Everything you do is a small step towards the next stage. For instance, we get rugs on them quickly, because that's a light form of pressure, and because they get used to someone standing on a crate to groom them, it introduces the idea of a rider being above them. You have to be very careful about introducing and fitting tack, because that's another area of pressure points. I'm always very fussy about fitting bridles, because of the pressure point behind the ears. Girthing up introduces another pressure and because you have to be careful not to tighten up the girth too much, I always use a breastgirth to help give security.

Things such as learning to be bathed are all part of the process of education.

I want the horse to be thinking forwards, so you have to make sure that weight and pressures are applied and adjusted gradually and only for short periods, or he will be thinking backwards instead. Being broken and introduced to work is obviously stressful, but you want it to be a positive, enjoyable form of stress rather than a negative one because then they're able to cope with the demands much more easily. We find that giving them a routine helps with this; right from the start the young horses will be turned out before or after they're worked and whatever way we start with, we carry on with.

Changes in routine start horses stressing. The routine of the whole yard is important, because that way they know everything that happens and what comes next. Although all the breakers work every day and go out in the field every day, if they start off being turned out in the morning and worked in the afternoon, that's the regime they'll stick too, and vice versa.

Rider fitness

Riding several horses each day plus competing keeps me fit. I don't have time to do anything else, though the nature of working with young horses means that you do a fair amount of walking.

9 Schooling and suppleness

S O WHAT DOES SCHOOLING have to do with getting a horse fit? The answer is more than you might imagine, because a horse who is able to carry himself in balance and is generally supple is better prepared to cope with the demands of his work, whether that be competing in a top-level endurance ride over varying terrain, jumping round a Newcomers course or completing a Pre-novice event. He will also be more likely to stay sound – because a horse can be physically fit but actually incapable of carrying out the job you ask him to do.

An increasing number of enlightened trainers are taking ideas from other disciplines, or, to borrow a phrase from the United States, cross-training. The benefits are so obvious that it seems remarkable that there are still a few diehards who cannot see the benefits of basic schooling for horses in all disciplines, from racing to endurance. But if, for instance, you are sending out a racehorse to run on a right-hand track, and he finds difficulty working on the right rein, it makes sense to sort out the problem on the flat and make him more manoeuvrable.

No matter how boring you find flatwork, it doesn't need to consist of going round in circles – though there are plenty of ways to do this and add variety, as mentioned later. A good trainer who understands your specialist discipline, if appropriate, will be able to suggest exercises and a schooling regime to improve your horse's way of going whilst keeping him interested. If you don't want to jump, working over ground-poles can bring enormous benefits; if you do, gridwork can improve your horse's balance, athleticism and enthusiasm. Even if you think you don't want to jump, don't discount it: work over small fences can reap big dividends and because the pre-set distances in gridwork take out the guesswork, you will find your confidence improves enormously.

Don't forget that flatwork (a less frightening term for those who are put off by the word 'dressage', even though its literal translation is simply 'training') doesn't have to be done within the confines of an arena. There is a lot you can do out hacking: transitions should have the same attention paid to them as in an arena, halts should be square, safe surroundings can provide opportunities for basic lateral work such as leg-yielding and so on.

The added bonus is that if you can get your horse listening to you out in the real world, you will have an advantage when it comes to competition. How many times do you hear people saying that their horses go beautifully at home in the school but go to pieces when in strange surroundings? If your horse learns to work wherever you ask him to, that shouldn't be so much of a risk.

For the horse who has been switched off by too frequent 'drilling' in an arena, a change of scene can work wonders. This can apply especially to native ponies, some of whom find school work a huge turn-off but can be schooled to go beautifully out hacking. Being out in the open tends to give them a bit more natural impulsion and you can teach all sorts of things, from walk to canter transitions to shoulder-in. Keep 'in the school' sessions occasional rather than regular – and add variety through the exercises you use, as shown below – and your competition dressage tests will often result in much higher marks.

Before you can school successfully, either in an arena or outside, you need to make sure that your horse is responsive and 'off the leg' – when you ask him to go forward, you want an instant response to a light aid, not one that comes five seconds later or not at all! One of the best trainers I have ever seen reckons that most riders work far harder than their horses, when it should be the other way round: but if you let yourself get into that situation, you can't blame the horse for taking the easy way.

I once saw Hannah Esberger-Shepherd, a talented young dressage rider and trainer, teach a group of riders who had won a lesson with her in a magazine competition. One arrived with a nice-looking young horse, a very long schooling whip and a long pair of spurs. The horse was very 'stuffy' and earthbound and Hannah's first step was to make the rider take off her spurs. She protested that without them, the horse wouldn't go and he certainly took very little notice of her aids.

Hannah got on board and asked the horse to move off from a light leg aid. When he took no notice, she gave him a sharp kick – and he was so shocked, he shot off in an energetic trot. Hannah was ready for this and did not lose her balance or restrict him with the reins. Next time, he was much more responsive and soon looked like a completely different horse. What had happened was an all-too-familiar scenario: the horse ignored his rider asking politely, so she fell into the trap of nagging with her legs and he simply switched off.

So don't assume that your horse will always be lazy. In a safe, enclosed area, ask him to go forward with a light aid and if he ignores you, give him a sharp kick or a sharp tap with a schooling whip. Praise him when he goes forward and don't be tempted to nag with your legs to keep the momentum going: he has to learn that you set the gait and tempo and he maintains them.

Useful flat exercises

When you're working on your own – and even if you're working with an instructor – it can be easy to fall into the trap of going round in circles. To keep a horse working well, you have to keep him thinking, so some of the following exercises might help you to add variety to your work as well as improving the way your horse goes. And whilst many of them do involve riding circles, there is enough variation within each exercise to keep you and your horse thinking!

Many of the exercises can be performed in the open, perhaps in a field, but you won't get the same degree of accuracy unless you mark out the points of a dressage arena. You don't necessarily have to use proper dressage markers with letters; cones, small drums or buckets will do the job as long as they are safely weighted down.

Warming up

Before your horse can perform well, he needs to warm up so that the muscles on both sides are worked evenly, so it is important to warm up and work on both reins equally. On a warm day, you can start with exercises in walk. In cold weather, if he's clipped, either use an exercise sheet to keep the muscles on his back, loins and hindquarters warm until you are ready to ask for more demanding work from him or – if he's fresh but not cold – go straight into rising (not sitting) trot, working in large circles and turns on both reins.

Figures based on curves

Serpentine warm-up in walk

This exercise is useful for both horse and rider, as it works the horse's muscles evenly and improves your aiding and balance. Establish a balanced, forward walk (don't ask for collection) and ride 5-m loops each side of the centre line, riding straight for two strides as you cross it and changing the bend before making your next loop. When you near the end of the arena, ride a 10-m circle onto the opposite rein.

Simple loops

Down the long side of the arena, ride shallow loops of 3 or 5 m. These can be ridden in walk, trot or canter; if ridden in canter, don't change leg and keep the bend over the leading leg.

Circles and spirals

Ride a 20-m circle in walk or trot, then gradually decrease the size to 10 or 15 m and leg-yield back out to a larger circle. This helps to get out of the trap of turning from the inside rein and means that the horse is encouraged to work from the inside leg to the outside hand.

Loops and circles

Start by riding a 10-m loop on the long side, then progressively add 10-m circles at the quarter markers and then the half marker (see Fig. 2). This exercise is excellent for improving suppleness and encouraging the horse to engage his hind legs. Start in walk or trot, which will be enough for a novice horse. An established horse who is capable of collection in canter should also be able to perform it in canter, incorporating simple or flying changes as appropriate – though in this gait, the exercise needs to be ridden in a 20 x 60 m arena to give more space.

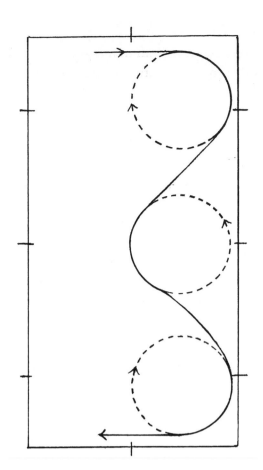

Fig. 2 The loops
and circles exercise.

Circles within circles

A variation on the previous exercise is to ride small circles within a 20-m
one. For instance, start at A and ride a 20-m circle, then ride a 10-m circle
at A, continue on your larger circle and ride another 10-metre one at X.
You can also incorporate 5-m circles, but these should only be ridden in
walk – and then only if within the capability of horse and rider. To keep
it interesting, vary the gait: you can have 20-m circles in walk, trot and
canter, 10-m circles in walk and trot and possibly 5-m circles in walk.
A horse who is fairly advanced in his training should eventually manage
10-m canter circles.

Circles and satellites

Try this exercise to develop rhythm, balance, engagement of the hind
legs and suppleness. Start by riding a 20-m circle from E or B, then ride

smaller satellite circles of 15 or 10 m off it by changing direction and bend as you leave the main circle and changing them again as you return to it. The main circle can be ridden in trot or canter and the satellite circles in walk or trot.

Lateral exercises

Turn on the forehand

The turn on the forehand – or turn about the forehand, as many trainers prefer to call it, as the last thing you want is for your horse to be actually on the forehand – is the easiest way to introduce lateral work. In this exercise, the horse is ridden forwards to a square halt, then asked to move his back end over, pivoting on the inside foreleg and crossing his inside hind leg in front of the outside one. The direction of the movement is defined by the front end, not the back: so in a turn on the forehand to the right, the horse will be flexed slightly right and his back end will move to the left. The rider's right leg will be the inside leg and the left leg, the outside one.

Apart from teaching the horse to move away from your leg, it is a good exercise for the horse who tries to 'hang' on the inside rein. Before you start trying to teach it from the saddle, teach your horse to move over in the stable by holding the headcollar rope with one hand to prevent him from moving forwards and nudging him with your hand on the girth whilst you give a voice command – 'over' is the logical one!

Until he gets the hang of it, it's best to have someone on the ground to help; your helper can gently prevent him from moving forward and, if necessary, nudge him over whilst you give the appropriate leg aid so he associates your aids with a signal he already knows. Some people prefer to use the leg behind the girth, whilst others believe it is better to use it on the girth.

Don't ask for more than one or two steps to start with and use a nudging 'on and off' leg aid rather than a constant pressure, as the latter will probably confuse him. As soon as he moves his back end in the required direction, give him a pat and ride forward to establish the momentum again.

Many horses find the movement easier on one rein than the other, so make allowances for this – and whilst you eventually want your horse to pivot around the inside leg without stepping forward, he might find it hard to understand that at first.

Leg-yielding

Leg-yielding is the logical progression from turn on the forehand and as well as improving engagement and suppleness, it helps to make the horse more responsive to the aids. Like turn on the forehand, it can be introduced at an early stage of the horse's education, as it does not need any degree of collection. The horse moves forward and sideways and should be almost straight, with just a small amount of flexion in his neck away from the direction of the movement – so if he is going forward and sideways to the left, his neck will be flexed very slightly right. (With the rider, the terms inside leg and inside hand apply to the way the horse is bent, so in the example above, the right leg and hand would be the inside ones.)

The easiest way to introduce leg-yielding is to turn down the three-quarter line, straighten the horse and ride straight for two or three strides, then ask for a tiny amount of flexion with the inside rein whilst keeping the horse forward and straight with the outside leg very slightly behind the girth. Apply the inside leg in a nudging movement on or slightly behind the girth to encourage him to move forwards and sideways. His natural inclination to go back to the track will encourage the desired response. Once the horse understands the exercise and will do it well on both reins, it is valuable sometimes to leg-yield *away from* the track.

One of the commonest problems is too much bend in the neck, which means the horse loses the forward movement and falls out through the shoulder – so if this happens, forget about asking for flexion, because you'll get a small amount just by thinking about it. There is no mystical element to this; it is simply that if you think about flexing left, your body and weight will mirror the thought. It is also important to keep a contact on the outside rein.

Once the horse has grasped the idea, try leg-yielding in trot, where you will find it easier to keep the forward momentum. Whatever gait you are working in, concentrate on quality rather than quantity, especially at first; it's better to get two or three good steps, ride forward and straight and then set up some fresh steps of leg-yielding, than to risk asking for too many steps at once. When you ask for too much, too soon, you are likely to end up doing an impression of a wiggly worm because you have lost the impulsion.

There are lots of exercises incorporating leg-yielding; for instance, you can ride a 20-m circle, spiral down to 15 m and leg-yield back out to the larger one. Another useful one is to ride straight down the centre of the school or schooling area, leg-yield halfway across then ride straight before leg-yielding again.

Shoulder-in

Shoulder-in is a great suppling exercise and it also helps in straightening a crooked horse – and it can be a useful way of getting a horse past a spooky object! As long as your horse can perform a 10-m circle – just in walk, to start with – he can be asked to start shoulder-in.

Shoulder-in encourages the horse to engage his inside hind leg and bend through his body. His inside foreleg crosses in front of the outside one and his inside hind leg steps forward and across under his body. Someone standing in front of the horse as the exercise is performed should see that the inside hind leg is in line with the outside foreleg.

Shoulder-in as required in competition is ridden at an angle of about 30 degrees from the track, but this is a lot to ask to start off with. With young and inexperienced horses, ask for a smaller angle, which is usually called position-in or shoulder-fore, which will also help in straightening him. When a horse is crooked, the temptation is to move the back end over, but it is only by positioning the shoulders correctly that you will be able to achieve straightness.

The easiest way to teach the beginnings of shoulder-in is to walk a 10-m circle in the corner of the school, then set off to ride down the long side feeling as if you are going to ride another circle of the same size. As you come out of your circle, use your inside leg on the girth to keep the horse going forward and his hind leg active, but keep your hands in the same position as when riding the circle; some trainers like to emphasize bringing the outside hand to the neck. If you get too much bend and

Shoulder-in is great for suppling and also for straightening a crooked horse. Michele Thorton schooling at the ILPH's Norfolk Centre.

lose the forward momentum – which is the commonest problem – think about using the outside rein but don't consciously use the inside one: you will still get minimum flexion even when you don't think you are asking for it.

Go for quality rather than quantity. When introducing shoulder-in, it is better to achieve a few good steps and then straighten the horse than to go on until things fall apart.

Poles and gridwork

Working over poles and through grids is essential for any horse who is expected to jump, but it can be equally important for horses and riders who don't have to – or don't want to – leave the ground. Ground-pole exercises can increase engagement of the hind legs, promote suppleness, improve reactions and add interest to your horse's work. Grids can achieve the same benefits and more: if you are trying to solve problems such as a dangling forefoot, a horse who jumps flat or veers to one side, gridwork supremo Carol Mailer has the answers. And if you thought gridwork was boring, think again, because it will keep you and your horse mentally active as well as giving you confidence.

Those who want to jump will obviously have no problem, but what about those who don't? The answer, says Carol – who helps riders ranging in experience and ability from Pony Club and Riding Club novices to international event riders – is to build grids comprising small cross-poles, so that the centre of the fence is barely off the ground – 23 cm (9 in) – and, to the horse, becomes an elevated canter stride. However, even 'barely there' fences such as this will ask him to look where he is going, improve his balance and reactions and flex his joints. The same also applies to the rider.

When you are working over fences, safety is important. Always try to have someone on the ground to adjust distances for you, as having to get on and off to do it yourself is time-consuming and breaks the rhythm of

Working over small fences can produce big benefits.

your work. (This applies to working over ground-poles, as well as actual jumping.) Be careful about the poles you use: Carol prefers to use light-weight ones made from special plastic by PolyJumps, as these won't hurt the horse if he hits them and are much easier to move and carry around.

Your horse should wear protective boots and Carol recommends that her clients use girths with built-in studguards even when their horses do not wear studs. The reason for this is that a careful horse who snaps up his forefeet may catch himself and the last thing you want is to punish him for jumping cleanly.

Poles on the ground

There are many exercises using poles on the ground that can be carried out on the lunge and under saddle. For a definitive guide, see *Schooling with Ground Poles*, by Claire Lilley.

With a young or novice horse who has not seen poles before, start by leading him over a pole on the ground in walk and progress to walking over poles set at random in your schooling area, so you incorporate turns and bends. Claire suggests that you can also lead him alongside poles, which will introduce the idea of working within dressage boards. Practise doing this on both reins, so that you can lead him from both sides. When he is confident, set out three poles 3.35–3.7 m (11–12 ft) apart, depending on the length of his stride. If he is a long-striding horse, the most comfortable distance for him will be 3.7–4 m (12–13 ft) and if he has a shorter stride, you will need to set them between 3 and 3.35 m (10–11 ft) apart. For bigger ponies, try setting the poles out at 2.75–3 m (9–10 ft) but reduce the distance for smaller ones. Carol Mailer points out that spacing the poles at this distance, rather than at particular intervals for walk, trot or canter, means that later you can work over them in all gaits under saddle without having to stop and alter them.

There are many variations of exercises that can be worked with ground-poles. For instance, the box of poles exercise, where four 3.7 m (12 ft) jump poles are laid on the ground to form a square, with a gap at each corner big enough for a horse to walk through, offers plenty of options. Walk in one corner and out through the other; turn and walk over a pole, then over the one opposite; walk in over a pole and halt in the centre of the box, and so on. With careful spacing, you can make a box that allows you to walk and trot over the poles and because the horse does not know where you are going to ask him to go next, it makes him listen to your aids. To keep the balance and rhythm and make your turns smoothly, you have to be clear and decisive, so the exercise offers a double benefit.

One of Claire's exercises for novice horses – and one which makes a good reinforcement and refresher for more established ones – is to set out four poles in a large star shape (see Fig. 3). As you ride a large circle around them, does your horse turn smoothly and in balance, or does he drift or wobble? Riding an accurate, balanced circle isn't as easy as good riders make it look, but this exercise will help: the key is to look where you are going, but to make sure that as you pass the end of each pole, your shoulders are in line with it.

Claire also uses poles laid out at random to improve transitions; as improving transitions will also improve engagement and balance, this is well worth doing. Claire advises riders to start in walk and walk up to each pole in turn; when the horse is right up to it with his forefeet

Fig. 3 The star exercise, using four ground-poles.

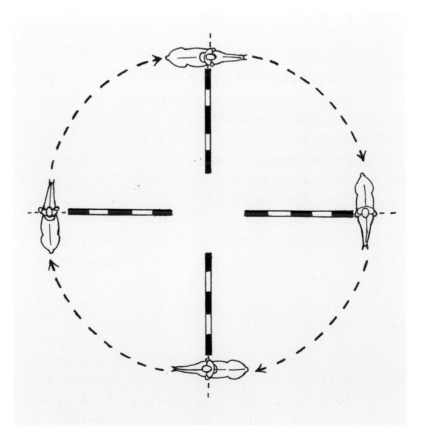

almost touching it, he should be asked to halt. Reward him by softening but not loosening the reins and repeat over the other poles.

Because the poles act as barriers, they encourage a precise halt, but if your horse is used to walking and trotting over them, he will probably overshoot. In this case, be careful to ask him to halt with your body, not simply through rein aids. When he responds, release your leg aids but stay sitting upright.

The next stage is to introduce trot and to ask for transitions to walk before the poles, allowing three strides of walk before the pole and only asking for trot again once the horse has walked over it. Ring the changes as you work – trot over a pole and go forward to walk after it, then halt before the next pole, walk over it and trot, and so on. The only limit to variation is your imagination.

As your horse's way of going improves, you can introduce direct transitions from halt to trot. Established horses can be asked to canter and to make transitions to trot using the poles, and those who are capable of walk to canter can be asked for direct transitions between these gaits. Working over poles is quite demanding for a horse, both mentally and physically, so it is important to allow him periods where he can relax.

If you want to encourage a horse to flex his joints, work from behind and use his shoulders, raised trotting poles can have a tremendous effect. These are simply poles with alternate ends raised about 15 cm (6 in) from the ground, over which the horse can be worked both on the lunge and under saddle. To introduce them, start with a line of three poles on the ground and work the horse over them, then raise one end of the last pole, then the opposite end of the middle pole, then raise the first pole. Eventually, you can build up to a line of five or six poles with alternately raised ends, but be careful not to overdo it, as this is hard work for a horse. You also need to have someone on the ground to replace any poles that are knocked out of place.

Cavalletti

The use of cavalletti was at one time a standard part of the education of any horse and rider but for some reason, went out of fashion in the UK. That seems to be changing and their value for groundwork is being recognized again; they make a natural progression from poles with alternately raised ends. However, for safety reasons they should not be stacked to make jumps as they do not fall cleanly and there is more likelihood of the horse being tripped than with conventional jump stands.

Cavalletti stands are traditionally made in the form of a cross, which allows them to be set at three heights between 15–20 cm (6–8 in), 30–35 cm (12–14 in) and 50 cm (20 in). The benefits of their use for training and fittening cannot be better expressed than this excerpt from Reiner Klimke's book, *Cavalletti*, first published by J.A. Allen in 1969 and subsequently updated. We might think that we have invented the idea of the holistic approach to riding and training, but Klimke – team gold medal winner at the 1964 Olympics, individual and team gold medal winner in 1984 and five times European dressage champion – took the 'whole horse' approach half a century ago:

> The education of a riding horse is the end sequel of a natural exercise. The horse's body has to be hardened and his muscles made flexible. Quite a proportional part of his training comes within the sphere of exercising the muscles and in this Cavalletti work is a valuable aid. The development of the muscles is dependent upon stimulation by exercise. They disappear if they are not used.
>
> This is why Cavalletti work is so exceptionally well suited to the development of the muscles, because it requires the horse to undergo disciplined exercise. The horse is forced to lift his feet higher than normal and therefore to put them down again on the ground more firmly and securely. All four legs and the muscles belonging to them are increasingly exercised, without the hoof beats in the three basic gaits being affected. The result of this is that important muscles used in all the horse's movements will be strengthened.
>
> If however Cavalletti work is overdone, or if the placing of each single rail is not suited to the horse's natural rhythm action, then there is the danger of serious injury. Muscles improve through exercise only when they are used appropriately to their position and their internal condition. They atrophy if they are compelled to undergo exercise in a false, cramped position, which they cannot properly execute. The results are swelling and debility caused by nutritive disturbances in the muscles. The reconstruction of new muscle matter cannot keep pace with the physiological obstruction, so the muscles deteriorate. Only

the systematic and slowly increased work over the Cavalletti can therefore accelerate the build-up of the horse's muscles.

It is also adapted to loosen up the muscles and to ease off stiffness, especially with over-worked horses. Horses which are ridden over Cavalletti with the neck in a lowered position, are able, for example, to arch their backs and thus relax the back muscles. The horse's movements return to their natural rhythm. And after a short time it is possible to see that the action from the hindquarters will be carried over to the forehand without hesitation, the horse's back oscillates and allows the rider to sit comfortably again. Of course rigid back muscles may be much improved anyway by riding on a loose rein and lowering the neck; but the correction is easier and simpler if Cavalletti are used because then the horse has his movements exactly regulated.

Thus work over Cavalletti has the advantage of loosening up and strengthening the horse's muscles. Obviously they are then useful for the development of both the heart and the circulation. It is enough to know that the exercise of all the organs affords training for the whole system and not just single parts of the body. The easy and constant increase of exercise improves the carrying capacity of the circulation and leads to the acquisition of stamina and condition.

Klimke preferred to start a horse working loose over cavalletti, having allowed him to warm up by cantering in the schooling area without side reins. Side reins were then fitted to the girth or roller, attached so that the line from bit to attachment was parallel to the ground and adjusted so that he could extend his neck forward and down and thus arch his back.

Gridwork for suppleness

Once your horse has progressed from walking, trotting and cantering over a single pole to working through five poles spaced as detailed earlier, you can start building a small grid. It is essential to have a helper on the ground to adjust distances and, because all exercises should be repeated on both reins, to re-build when necessary.

The first step is to replace the last ground-pole with a small cross-pole fence, so that the centre of the cross – where you want him to jump – is about 23 cm (9 in) high. Approach in trot to start with and ride down the line of poles exactly as you did before, keeping your legs on to maintain impulsion.

The horse might pop over the cross-pole, or he might simply take a bigger trot stride. If the worst comes to the worst, he might stop: in this case, don't let him turn away and quietly insist that he steps over it. Once he is coping happily with this, replace the third pole with a cross-pole and you will find that as he lands, his momentum should carry him into a nice round canter stride – thanks to the fourth pole on the ground – and over the second cross-pole. Next, turn the first pole on the ground into a cross-pole and approach as before, from trot. If he is still trotting over the fences rather than making a proper jump, Carol Mailer advises raising the ends of the third cross-pole so that the angle of the cross is more acute; the height will barely alter, but the appearance will encourage him to pick up more.

Don't try to do too much in one session and always end on a good note. Next time, warm up and repeat your earlier work, then approach in canter. Think about rhythm and balance and if the horse rushes, revert to trot until he gains confidence to keep his rhythm in canter, too.

Always work on both reins and make sure you ride at least three straight strides away from the final cross-pole; don't let your horse 'fall in a heap' once he gets to the other side. Once you have made a straight, calm, getaway, ride a good turn and make sure it is you who decides which way you are going.

If you want to develop your grid, do it in easy stages and always start by approaching in trot. Start by adding a horizontal pole behind the last cross-pole; it should be just slightly higher than the centre of the cross and give a spread of about 60 cm (2 ft). Remember that when you add poles behind, you need to adjust the distances in your grid so that the non-jumping strides remain the same. When the horse is going calmly and confidently through the grid on both reins, add a horizontal pole to the first cross-pole in the same way. To end this next phase, turn the centre cross-pole into an upright that is the same height as the horizontal pole on the cross fences, with a pole on the ground just in front of it to act as a groundline.

So far, so good? Then at your next gridwork session – these can be incorporated into your schooling two or three times a week – work through the earlier stages and turn the last fence into a small ascending oxer by adding a slightly lower pole in front of your upright. For those who want to progress further, fence heights can be raised gradually and you can also introduce a bounce fence at the start of the grid.

Fences on a circle

Once a horse is jumping happily through small grids, one of the most valuable exercises you can do is also one of the simplest – but doing it correctly isn't as easy as it sounds! Build a 60 cm (2 ft) high fence on a 20-m circle. When your horse is warmed up and you have both got your eye in with a little gridwork, canter the circle and aim to meet the fence on a regular, rhythmical stride.

The idea of this exercise is to prevent riders 'over-riding' a fence and to encourage the horse to keep a rhythm. When you are happy with one fence, build another on the opposite side of the circle and keep the same priorities.

It is important to do this exercise on both reins. Because of its basic aims, hopefully, your horse will stay calm. If he does start to rush, move away from the fences and work in canter on both reins, both on circles and going large, returning calmly to the fences for one or two circuits when he is settled. If he does not know when he is going to be asked to work on the flat and when you are going to incorporate the fences, he will be less likely to anticipate or rush.

10 Hands on

GETTING YOUR HORSE fit demands, as we've already seen, a holistic approach that ranges from his actual work to the fit of his tack and even his rugs. There are also many ways in which you can help to maintain his physical and mental well-being, from grooming, massage and stretching techniques to complementary therapies. In some cases, you can carry out 'support work' for your horse yourself but in others, it is important to call in a qualified practitioner who will work with your vet's permission.

Whilst techniques such as stretches and therapies such as magnotherapy can be of great benefit, they also have the potential to do harm if carried out in the wrong way and/or in the wrong circumstances. If you think your horse has a problem, your starting point must always be veterinary advice. Most vets are, thankfully, much more open-minded than was perhaps the case at one time and appreciate the benefit that can be obtained from the work of chartered physiotherapists, qualified chiropractors and osteopaths and so on. What they do not appreciate, and what no horse owner should condone or subject their horse to, is unqualified 'back people' and others who lack not only proper training but often other essentials such as proper insurance.

Grooming and strapping

Although grooming can't play an active role in keeping your horse fit, it certainly contributes to his well-being and your assessment of it: it is much more than just a matter of appearances. It can tell you how your horse is feeling – physically and mentally – allow you to spot potential problems and, if you incorporate some simple stretch or massage techniques, help you to keep him supple. And if you're trying to encourage correct muscle build-up on a young or unfit horse, you can take grooming a step further. The traditional technique where muscles on the neck and quarters are 'banged' with a straw wisp or leather pad, is enjoying a revival.

Opinion varies on whether or not grooming offers actual benefits to the horse's skin and coat. There's undoubtedly a lot of truth in the old saying that it's what you put on the inside that counts, rather than what you do to the outside, but the extra benefits are well worth the elbow grease. Linda Tellington-Jones, founder of the Tellington Touch technique, says that a well-mannered horse should stand quietly whilst being groomed and allow himself to be touched anywhere – even on sensitive or vulnerable areas such as the ears, nostrils and girth areas. However, she points out that most horses have places they don't like to be touched and can only show this by tensing muscles, moving around or even kicking out.

So use grooming time to 'read' your horse. If he flinches or ducks down when you groom the area under or behind the saddle, check your saddle fit; if he lays back his ears or tries to nip when you brush the girth area, check for signs of soreness in muscles or skin. In both cases, you may need professional help. Common sense dictates that some horses are more sensitive than others. Those with a lot of Thoroughbred or Arab blood tend to be thin-skinned and may find ordinary grooming brushes too harsh. If a horse is punished for reacting to discomfort, he soon associates grooming with discomfort.

This creates a vicious circle, so if you have a horse who has been in previous homes and hates being groomed, adapting your methods might help. Using an extra soft brush – goats' hair brushes are amongst the gentlest – or simply your hands may enable him to accept grooming as a pleasurable process. Using your hands is a form of massage and simply using firm stroking movements can help your horse relax. Copy the grooming techniques horses themselves use out in the field: scratch the withers area and the top of the tail, but watch out in case your horse decides to return the favour by grooming you!

Read any of the old books on looking after horses and you'll see suggested timetables of daily care that include half an hour to 'quarter' the horse before exercise and an hour's strapping afterwards. Although few people have the time to carry out those regimes now, there are points that can be borrowed from them. Quartering means giving the horse a brush over before exercise to make him presentable and gets its name from the way the old grooms used to fold back the rugs to brush a quarter of the horse at a time. Proper grooming or strapping was done after exercise, when it was more effective because the muscles were warm and the blood was nearer the surface.

In 1937 D. W. Brock, the author of a book called *Stablecraft*, detailed the purpose of grooming as 'the drying of the skin, should it be wet from sweat or rain; the cleaning of the skin and the removal of scurf and dandruff; the massage of the skin and muscles'. The secret, he revealed, was in the correct use of a body brush:

> It is not sufficient merely to pat the brush on to the horse. The secret of successful grooming is to force the brush, with all the weight of your body and the strength of your arm behind it, through the coat. For that reason you should stand right away from the horse so that you can lean your full weight on to the brush as you push it through the coat. You must not bang the brush down when you put it on the horse at the beginning of each stroke; you must lay it gently on the horse and then put your weight on it and force it through the coat.

This technique is as relevant today as it was then. Whilst few of us could match the old grooms for the amount of time or technique they put into grooming their charges, an extra thorough grooming whenever you can make time will benefit your horse physically and mentally: a bath and some spray-on coat sheen might make him look as clean, but he won't get the same benefits.

Grooming can be taken a step further by 'banging' muscles on the neck and quarters with a leather pad. Start gently, then build up the force as the horse gets used to it – eventually, you'll often find he leans into the impact of the pad. It has to be done regularly to see an effect, but really does help build up the muscles. What happens is that the muscles contract as the horse anticipates the pad coming down, then relax. It's a technique that show pony producers Stuart, Nigel and Penny Hollings use to great effect.

Keep all your senses alert whilst you're grooming your horse. Do you notice slight indications of heat and swelling? Are his shoes secure, with no risen clenches? Does he seem his usual self, or is he a bit grumpy or off-colour? Time spent grooming is never wasted. Even if your horse lives out and needs the grease left in his coat as protection against the weather, he'll benefit from the attention and you'll spot any nicks or skin problems as soon as they arise.

As well as keeping your horse clean, keep your grooming equipment up to scratch. Dirty brushes mean a dirty horse no matter how much elbow grease you put in and they can also spread infection. And if you're tempted by high-tech grooming machines, think twice. They might save time – and can be a good way of desensitizing horses who are nervous of being clipped – but they can't compare with the hands-on approach for judging how your horse feels.

Massage

Grooming is in itself a form of massage, but 'proper' massage is an art and a skill that, when carried out correctly, can have a real impact on a horse's physical and mental well-being. There are now many massage therapists who make regular visits to equine athletes in all disciplines; as always, before letting someone attend to your horse, check his or her qualifications and training as it is important that they have a good understanding of anatomy. For a start, anyone carrying out massage must be able to identify and avoid areas where bone protuberances are just under the skin, such as the stifle joint, the point of the elbow and the point of the hip.

You can also learn massage techniques yourself but although these can be used both before and after exercise, they can't develop muscle strength. The best way to learn effective massage techniques is to attend a course run by a qualified practitioner; for instance, in the UK, they are run by the renowned chartered physiotherapist Mary Bromiley. It is also important to recognize cases when massage should not be applied – for instance, to a horse with a skin condition such as ringworm or one suffering from lymphangitis. Although it might seem like a simple and beneficial activity, massage can be harmful when practised in the wrong circumstances and is only effective if the right techniques are employed.

Mechanical massagers range from hand-held units to high tech (and high priced!) equipment which is fastened on to the horse. Most notable is probably the Equissage system, a favourite of many competition riders and used to great effect at the ILPH (see the Case History at the end of Chapter 1.)

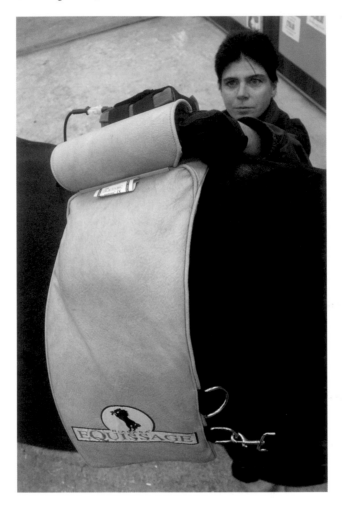

The Equissage massage system is used successfully by the ILPH.

Stretches

Basic stretching exercises that can be easily incorporated into your daily routine – perhaps after you have finished grooming or before you ride – can help keep your horse limber. In fact, you may already be doing this without realizing it: by gently extending the forelegs after you have girthed up to make sure the skin around the girth and elbows areas is not being pinched, you are performing a gentle stretch. The ones recommended below are simple stretches that should benefit any horse, but the information is offered as a guideline rather than a DIY manual. As you'll know if you've done it yourself, over-extending a limb's range of movement can cause discomfort or even damage and if your horse reacts by pulling against you, you are both at risk. The best way to learn how to carry out stretches is to get a qualified person such as a chartered physiotherapist to demonstrate; if that isn't possible, be cautious with the limb stretches – make sure that you are encouraging the horse to stretch rather than pulling his limb into a position he finds uncomfortable.

This warning obviously doesn't apply so much to the first two stretches, the carrot stretch and the belly lift, because the horse does the work himself in reaction to a stimulus. But even with these, you need to be careful: suddenly exerting pressure on a horse's midline might encourage him to lift his back, but with an accompanying kick out! It is also important to build up the range of his stretch gradually if he seems to find it difficult to, say, make a carrot stretch back to his hip. If he shows any sign of discomfort, stop the exercise and get veterinary advice. All the stretches mentioned here can be performed twice (on each side, where appropriate) and carried out daily.

Carrot stretches

These should be done whilst you hold the horse on a loose headcollar rope. Take a carrot or other reward and hold it at the horse's shoulder, so he has to turn his head and neck round to reach it. If he finds this easy, encourage him to stretch round further by moving the carrot back towards his hip.

To encourage him to stretch his topline and raise his back, hold the carrot between his front legs so he has to stretch down and round.

Belly lift

We often talk about wanting the horse to round and lift his back under the rider – but to do this, he has to be able to lift his abdominal muscles. The best exercise for encouraging this is to run your fingers along the midline of his belly, using a firm pressure, but be conscious of the risks – a horse who is ticklish might react by cow-kicking. If your horse's range of motion is particularly limited, it's worth getting him and the fit of your saddle checked.

Pick out stretch

Although you may see this stretch referred to by other names, calling it the pick out stretch makes it easier to remember – because you start by picking up a foreleg as if you were going to pick out the horse's hoof. Support it at the fetlock, then gently draw it back, keeping the cannon bone parallel to the ground. This can be carried out on the hind legs in a similar way, drawing the leg back gently and slowly.

Crossover stretch

Pick up a front leg and, standing in front of and slightly to one side of the horse, move it gently across until the hoof is at a point perpendicular to the centre of the chest. This will help free up the muscles of the shoulders and chest.

Hamstring stretch

Pick up a hind leg and, standing in front and slightly to one side, gently advance it towards the foreleg on the same side. By doing this, you increase the mobility of the hind legs; it is excellent for jumpers and for helping the horse's capability to take more weight on his hind legs.

Magnotherapy

Magnotherapy, part of the regime of many top competition horses as well as being used for rehabilitation and relaxation, has gone mainstream. Once classified as 'alternative' or 'complementary', it is now an accepted therapy not just for horses with problems, but as a way of promoting general well-being. The use of magnets to promote healing was recognized in ancient Chinese medicine and today, we have everything from magnetic rugs to boots and even bridle inserts.

In the 1960s, astronauts in weightless conditions suffered nausea and weight loss. German biophysicist Wolfgang Ludwig discovered that magnetic therapy countered this; further research showed that there were other health benefits and equipment with pulsed electrical magnetic fields was used in hospitals.

In simple terms, magnetic therapy is said to stimulate circulation and thus have a healing effect. The magnetic field improves the transfer of substances via the blood cells, speeding up the delivery of oxygen and nutrients. At the same time it helps the removal of toxins via the lymphatic system. There are two kinds of magnetic field: a pulsed electro-magnetic field, which needs a supply of electricity, and a static one, which doesn't. Pulsed electro-magnetic field therapy (PEMFT) is often said to be more effective and has a variable frequency; higher frequencies are often used to reduce initial pain after an injury and are followed by a lower frequency to continue the healing process.

At first, many people dismissed this as mumbo-jumbo, but a high-profile case in 1982 raised greater awareness. Police horse Sefton received terrible injuries in the Hyde Park bombing and was treated by animal physiotherapist Sherry Scott, who explained that in qualified hands, PEMFT could help with wounds that had been stitched by preventing swelling and thus stopping the stitches giving way.

Some PEMFT systems are incorporated into rugs, using an electrical supply. Research using thermography (heat scanning) and scintigraphy (which uses radioactive markers) shows that the beneficial effects are more than imagined; thermography has been used to measure an increase in blood flow and scintigraphy has demonstrated a significant increase in the rate at which substances taken into the soft tissues are taken up by the body.

In some situations, the need for electricity means that PEMFT is not practical. This is when static field products, such as rugs, horse boots, dog collars and wristbands for riders, may help. There are also many arguments about the type and strength of magnets that should be used, so if you are thinking of buying a large item such as a magnetic rug, you may want to take advantage of the 'hire before you buy' offers made by some companies. Anecdotal evidence suggests that static field products can be especially useful in some cases of arthritis, perhaps by reducing muscle tension.

So when can magnetic therapy help? In general, if improved circulation would benefit a condition, it could be worth trying if your vet approves – so frequent candidates include horses suffering from ligament and tendon injuries, those who have newly formed splints and animals who could benefit from increased blood flow before exercise. It must be stressed that magnotherapy should not be used as a first attempt to promote healing: it should only be used after veterinary advice has been sought. There have been reports of, for instance, misguided owners using magnetic boots on horses who have actually suffered a limb fracture.

Opinions vary as to whether there are instances where magnetic therapy should not be used, which makes it even more important to get your vet's advice. For instance, some practitioners say it should not be used on pregnant mares or haemotomas, whilst others believe that this applies only to PEMFT.

McTimoney chiropractic and EMRT

It would not be fair to say that one 'hands-on' technique is better than another, as so much depends on what you are trying to achieve and, of course, the experience of the individual practitioner. For instance, many veterinary practices work with chartered physiotherapists – particularly those who are members of the Association of Chartered Physiotherapists in Animal Therapy (ACPAT) and osteopaths. The essential issues are that the practitioner holds a recognized qualification and public liability insurance, has a good knowledge of horses and works under the guidance of your veterinary surgeon; legally, the need for veterinary approval applies even to massage therapists.

However, there are two approaches which seem to be becoming particularly popular with horse owners and which are also reported by many to achieve good results, perhaps in part owing to the fact that they are readily accepted by animals. One is McTimoney chiropractic and the other, Equine Muscle Release Therapy (EMRT).

McTimoney is a form of chiropractic manipulation often used to help back, neck, pelvic and musculoskeletal problems. It aligns and balances the musculoskeletal system, with a particular focus on the spine and pelvis, and practitioners work to eliminate the cause of a problem where possible, not just to treat the symptoms.

EMRT is a relatively new approach and was developed for horses from the original Bowen Technique – devised by Tom Bowen in Australia – by Alison Goward. It involves a series of gentle moves, made over muscles in specific areas, in a particular sequence, which signal the brain to take the spasm out of those muscles. I have seen EMRT practitioner Lesley Bayley achieve excellent long-term results when other approaches have failed. One of Lesley's cases was a dressage horse who, after he had been grazing for 20 minutes, hurtled round the field bucking and kicking – not in high spirits, but in distress. This happened repeatedly and the owner's vet could find no explanation so, with his permission, Lesley was called in. When she treated the horse, she found that he was very tight over his topline, especially in the lumbar area. Next morning he was turned out to graze and 20 minutes later, everyone was waiting for the usual explosion. The horse simply carried on grazing and there has been no repeat of his behaviour; Lesley believes that something was trapped and caused pain, either as a result of or exacerbated by the head-down position, and the treatment released it.

With the best will in the world, everything we do to our horses puts pressure on them. They are not designed to carry saddles on their backs, let alone the sometimes considerable weight of their riders. Sometimes, even when riders are careful to warm up and cool down and to allow periods of relaxation during concentrated schooling, muscles may become overworked in the same way that, if we sit too long in front of a computer or drive for long periods, we may end up with aching backs, necks, or shoulders. A good practitioner – whether a chartered physio-therapist, an osteopath, a McTimoney chiropractor or whatever – can therefore be a valuable member of the support team for anyone getting a horse fit and trying to keep him in, literally, good working order.

Horse walkers and treadmills

Horse walkers and treadmills, in particular the former, have become standard equipment on many yards. Their value is more for loosening up than for actual fittening, though treadmills with adjustable speeds can be used at trot as well as walk speeds and thus may have more of a fittening benefit. Some, such as those in equine veterinary research institutes, can be geared up to full gallop speed when horses are being evaluated for respiratory conditions.

Opinions vary as to whether walkers or treadmills are better. Some experts believe that treadmills are preferable because the horse is working on a straight line, though the general opinion is that so long as horses on walkers are worked equally on both reins, they are of equal value. The key factor about both is that they should be used in addition to correct work, not instead of it.

Hydrotherapy

Human athletes have learned to appreciate the benefits of training and rehabilitation aids such as treadmills and hydrotherapy. Now equine athletes can share their advantages at the increasing number of equine 'spas', with facilities ranging from swimming pools to water treadmills. Harnessing the power of water isn't, of course, a new idea: equine swimming pools have been part of some racing yards' regimes for many years and Ginger McCain, who trained the legendary three times Grand National winner Red Rum, credited being able to work him on the sand and in the sea as the saviour of the horse's soundness.

A horse walker can be beneficial when used as well as, not instead of, correct work.

Views on whether swimming horses in pools gets them fit for racing, eventing or endurance varies; one leading eventing vet reckons that it

gets them fit for swimming, but for little else! However, water treadmills, which were first used in America, are generally recognized as a different proposition. One of the first to be used commercially in the UK is housed in a large barn and set in a curving basin. The horse walks into a water channel and onto the treadmill, but because the exit is not straight in front of him, he is not tempted to try to rush out.

A 16 hh horse is working in about 1.22 m (4 ft) of water at its standard setting, though the level can be altered according to the size of the animal. There are also eight jacuzzi jets which can be turned on for a horse with specific problems, such as tendon injuries. Temperature is regulated and when a horse comes out after an average 20-minute session he is dried off under heat lamps.

When a horse is walked on the treadmill, the buoyancy factor reduces his effective weight by up to 45 per cent. This means that the horse's muscles and cardiovascular system can be worked without putting strain on the joints. Some vets believe that water treadmills are better than swimming pools because when a horse swims, he uses different muscles from when he gallops, and a swimming horse also holds his breath, whilst a water treadmill works the same muscles as are used on land and the horse breathes normally.

You too!

Although many riders are prepared to do anything to help their horses, often at great expense, they are not so ready to look after themselves. But it is just as important to make sure that you are fit, sound and in physical symmetry, because a rider problem can also become a horse problem. As explained in the next chapter, it goes beyond basic physical fitness – so when you get your horse checked, do the same for yourself.

11 Fit to ride

WHILST MANY RIDERS are concerned about getting their horses fit, relatively few pay the same attention to their own needs; there is a common but only partially correct assumption that regular riding and all the work associated with looking after a horse are all that is needed to keep you in good shape. This will certainly play a major part – because with people, as with horses, fitness regimes need to be sport-specific to a certain degree – but it may not be enough. Even professional riders who ride several horses a day may have areas that can be improved; the majority of owners who ride for pleasure and may not even be able to ride one horse every day certainly will.

Fitness and health go hand in hand for humans as much as they do for horses. Just being with, caring for and riding a horse offers real benefits, as most of us know. There is immense satisfaction in knowing that you can keep an animal healthy and happy and the benefits that horses give to us in offering different challenges and different escapes from the demands of daily life are enormous. Whether you have a demanding job outside the home or equally demanding family commitments within it – or even both – the chance and the need to set those stresses on one side whilst you focus on your horse is irreplaceable. Lord Palmerston hit the nail on the head when he said, 'The best thing for the inside of a man is the outside of a horse' and you only have to look at the work of organizations such as The Fortune Centre for Riding Therapy and Riding for the Disabled to see how horses can literally change lives.

But whether your horse therapy is based on the challenge of competition or the chance to unwind on a leisurely hack, you owe it to your horse to build and maintain your own physical fitness and balanced state of mind. For a start, it could prevent accidents, as Dr David Marlin points out. At a 1990 conference attended by many international riders, he and his team asked them how concerned they were about their horses' welfare in advance of Atlanta and the majority said they were very concerned – but when asked about their own welfare, they did not have the same worries. But as Dr Marlin explains, tired, heat-stressed, disorientated riders make mistakes as well as tired, heat-stressed, disorientated horses. As he spells out: it doesn't matter who makes the mistake if it results in a horse and rider falling.

Even at less exalted levels, inadequate rider fitness or physical problems can have a bad effect on the horse and set up a whole range of problems. My own example proves this: as this book was in preparation I knew that I was riding out of balance, putting more weight on my right stirrup than my left despite all my efforts to stay in balance. It was a chicken and egg scenario: was the problem caused by me, my saddle, my young horse seemingly finding it more difficult to stay straight on the left rein or a combination of all three, made worse at the time by getting bucked off?

The first step was to call in Mark Fisher, a Society of Master Saddlers qualified saddle fitter who is also an accomplished rider with a great understanding of the way horses and riders work. Mark appreciated my problem and said that whilst he could balance my air-flocked saddle to raise my right seatbone very slightly and thus correct my imbalance, I needed to start by getting myself checked and, if necessary, treated to see if that could solve or help my problem. We had already confirmed that my mare was not stiff or sore and had a good range of movement through her back.

The next stage was to visit Bruce Smart, a qualified osteopath and sports injury therapist. Bruce found that my involuntary dismount had caused temporary problems, but that I also had long-term ones caused by general wear and tear and occupational hazards. Everyone has them, but mine were not helped by the fact that I had once broken my right collarbone and as a result my scapula 'winged out' and by the fact that I spend long periods at a word processor, albeit whilst paying care to seat position and all the other considerations that come under the label of workplace ergonomics.

After one session with Bruce, the tension in my right shoulder and arm were greatly reduced and I could look over my right shoulder without discomfort – something which had gradually got worse and which I had taken for granted. Two more treatments improved things even more. Mark was then able to adjust my saddle to compensate for the remaining imbalance that I will probably always have and to lift it slightly at the back so that it was no longer tipping me back slightly and I could sit centrally without fighting it; the adjustments were tiny, but made a huge difference.

The immediate result was that I felt more secure and stable and no longer felt constant tension across my lower back. I could also transfer my weight evenly down through both sides of my body – and my 'crooked' 4-year-old was suddenly much straighter. If your weight moves to one side, your horse will move to catch you up, which is great when you want sideways movement and can ask for it deliberately, but not so great when it's unintentional. Just as important, equine vertical or sideways take-offs are much easier to sit!

If you're trying to get fitter, treat yourself with the same consideration as your horse by building up gradually. If you are overweight or have any medical conditions, it's a good idea to get your doctor's advice first. If you smoke – and it's amazing how many top-class riders are still addicted to the killer weed – then do yourself and those who care about you a favour and make a real effort to give up.

Weighty matters

It's often said that one of the greatest health dangers facing modern generations – particularly in the USA but also in the UK – is obesity. There are probably relatively few obese riders, but there are certainly plenty who are not at their optimum weight. This does not mean that you need to be supermodel slim, but it does mean that you need to be able to give yourself and your horse the best chance of moving and reacting efficiently. Dressage rider and trainer Pammy Hutton expressed this beautifully when she confessed that she knew that she rode well at 70 kg (10 st 4 lb) but was less effective at a stone (6.35 kg) heavier. It is not that she is too heavy for her horses at the upper weight, but that she knows the level at which she feels and rides best.

Having said that, riders who know they are overweight and buy a horse who is supposedly up to it perhaps need to re-think. A horse's weight-carrying ability is often defined according to the amount of bone he has; bone is measured round the widest part of the front cannon bone, just below the knee and as an example, the British Show Hack, Cob and Riding Horse Association rules say that a lightweight show cob should have a minimum of 21.6 cm (8½ in) of bone and be capable of carrying 89 kg (14 stone) whilst a heavyweight should have a minimum of 23 cm (9 in) and be capable of carrying a greater weight. However, there is more to it than this, since overall conformation must also be taken into account: a well-made horse with short cannon bones is a better proposition than one with less good conformation and/or relatively long cannon bones, even if the actual bone measurement of the latter is higher.

However, no matter how solidly built a horse, or how much bone he has, the fact remains that he still has to carry a rider on his back – and the horse's back is not designed to bear large loads. Overweight riders are also less likely to be agile and to 'ride light', though there are some exceptions. If this is starting to make you feel guilty, do yourself and your horse a favour and shed some excess weight; he will certainly appreciate it and so will you. Overweight horses are more likely to suffer from problems ranging from being out of breath to overloaded joints, and so are overweight riders.

Although you don't usually need a chart to know if you are overweight, medical and fitness experts now point to a system called the body mass index (BMI). This is because frame size varies – some of us are natural Thoroughbreds and others, natural cobs – and as such it is better to aim for a weight range rather than a specific weight for a specific height. A quick internet search for BMI will find you instant calculators that enable you to type in your height and find your optimum weight range, but if you prefer to calculate manually, use the following formula:

- Work out your height in metres and square it (multiply the figure by itself).

- Find your weight in kilograms.

- Divide your weight by your squared height.

For example, if you are 1.6 m (5 ft 3 in) and weigh 57 kg (9 st), the equation would be: 1.6 x 1.6 = 2.56, so your BMI is 57 divided by 2.56 = 22.

The accepted BMI scale is:

Underweight – BMI less than 18.5

Ideal – BMI 18.5–25

Overweight – BMI 25–30

Obese – BMI 30–40

Very obese – BMI greater than 40

In our example, you would be in the ideal category. However, if you are 1.6 m (5 ft 3 in) and weigh 65 kg (10 st) your BMI would be 25.39 and you would have moved into the overweight category.

Some words of warning about the BMI index: if you are already an athlete or are well muscled – and please don't kid yourself by fondly imagining that fat is muscle – it will not be as accurate, since muscle weighs more than fat and the calculation can shift you into the next category even if you have an acceptable level of body fat. It should also not be used as a guideline for pregnant or breast-feeding women.

If you need to lose weight, the only effective way is combining healthy eating patterns with exercise to achieve a gradual weight loss of 0.5–1 kg (1–2.2 lb) per week. Crash or gimmicky diets may see you losing a lot more weight very quickly, but won't have the same long-term beneficial effect. Whether you go it alone or opt for support in numbers by joining a slimming club, keep in mind the following list of government/World Health Organization healthy eating guidelines. The best thing about them is that they are easy to follow and don't mean you have to deprive yourself, unless you are addicted to fatty meat and fried foods!

Most of us need to eat less saturated fats, sugar and salts and more fruit and vegetables – and couple this with an active lifestyle. It is now recommended that everyone eats five portions of fruit and vegetables a day; one portion can be defined as:

Three heaped tablespoons of vegetables (any kind).

One dessert bowlful of mixed salad – but if you're trying to lose weight, remember that ordinary salad dressings can contain an enormous number of hidden calories.

Half a grapefruit or avocado.

One apple, banana, orange or other citrus fruit.

Two plums or similar sized fruits.

A handful of grapes, cherries or berries.

One tablespoon of dried fruit such as raisins or apricots.

One 150 ml glass (5 fl oz) of 100 per cent fruit juice without added sugar.

Many people shy away from eating bread, potatoes, rice and pasta if they are trying to lose weight, but this can be a mistake as they are good sources of fibre. And although we need to cut down on saturated fats, a completely fat-free diet – unless specifically prescribed by your doctor because of a medical condition – is a mistake, as some contain vitamins and other essentials. Fish is a valuable addition to any diet and if you don't like it, you should think about taking supplements such as cod liver oil.

The biggest fatty dangers come from hidden fats. It's easy to spot it on meat, but there are a lot of hidden fats in foods such as pies, pastries and meat products such as sausages, burgers and convenience foods with sauces. The moral is to read the label before you buy!

Salt is another nutritional danger area. The recommended daily intake for an adult is 6 g per day, which is easily met by salt occurring naturally in foods; most of us take in more than this. Apart from cutting down on the salt used in cooking – a little goes a long way and herbs and spices add just as much flavour as a heavy hand on the salt shaker – be careful to read food labels again. Commercial soups, sauces and convenience meals often have high levels of salt.

The dehydration factor

Dehydration is a factor with riders just as much as with horses. Most of us underestimate the amount of water we need to drink – because if you feel thirsty, you're already dehydrated – and the results can range from tiredness and headaches to lack of co-ordination. As a guideline, we need to take in about 2 litres (3½ pints) per day, though this includes water available through food; a lot of people start off trying to actually drink this quantity of water per day and find it impossible, for obvious physical reasons! But if you aim to drink 1½ litres (2⅔ pints) of water and drink small amounts regularly, perhaps by keeping a bottle on your desk, you'll find it easier.

The emphasis is on water as opposed to ordinary tea and coffee as too much caffeine – present in both – will result in dehydration. This applies even more to alcohol. No one has to give up their favourite cup or tipple, but keep alcohol consumption to within recommended limits and if you're one of those who likes regular cups of tea or coffee, try switching to decaffeinated. The easiest way, if you need a kick-start in the morning from the real thing, is to switch to decaffeinated after lunch, so long as you don't cheat by getting in as much of the 'real thing' as possible first! The good news, if you haven't tried them, is that there are decaffeinated brands now available with just as much flavour as the ordinary kind and you might find that you come to prefer them.

If you overdo it, especially on a hot day, compensate quickly by dissolving a sachet of rehydration salts – electrolytes available from any chemist – in a glass of water. Commercial sports drinks are available, but these often have very high sugar levels. Independent nutritionist Clare MacLeod suggests making your own by mixing 200 ml (8 fl oz) fruit squash (not the sugar-free version, as you need a certain amount of sugar for this purpose) with water and adding a quarter of a teaspoon of salt.

Fitness options

There are lots of ways to improve and maintain your general fitness and no such thing as a right or a wrong way – the one that works for you is the one you enjoy, because that means you'll stick at it. So whilst some people enjoy the social atmosphere of the gym or fitness class, others prefer to work alone or simply to go walking with a good companion, whether human or canine!

The good news is that if you look after a horse, the chances are that you are fairly active. A base level of health is that you should be able to manage 30 minutes of moderate activity a day – not necessarily all in one go. By the time you've factored in mucking out, leading your horse down to the field, proper grooming and all the other things that make up being a DIY owner, you've got a start on most non-horsy people. Add in a good walk with a dog and you're more than halfway there. If you're trying to lose weight, being around horses will help: it has been estimated that mucking out burns up to 480 calories per hour, sweeping 400, hacking 240 and schooling 350; unfortunately no one has worked out how many the horse uses!

However, health is not the same as fitness, even though they usually go together. Health can be defined as being free from and resilient to disease whilst fitness, as we have already seen with horses, means being capable of doing a specific job – so being truly fit to ride demands a bit more. A good rule of thumb is that you should exercise at least three times a week, for one 30-minute or two 15-minute sessions, at an intensity that raises your heartbeat; you should feel that you are out of breath, but not to the extent that you can't hold a conversation.

There is not the scope in this book to go into human fitness in detail, but walking, cycling, swimming and skipping can be used to great effect. Never underestimate the value of walking: one leading cardiologist says that brisk walking for 45 minutes a day, four days per week, will produce a fat loss of 8 kg (18 lb) in one year provided there are no changes to the diet. Walking not only improves cardiovascular fitness, it may even improve bone density and because it is a low-impact form of exercise, will not stress your joints as much as running or jogging. Skipping also benefits the heart and lungs, but has a higher impact – though it will only be carried out for short periods – and cycling can work heart, lungs and muscles. If you're a cross-country enthusiast, try cycling whilst standing on the pedals rather than sitting on the seat – commonly known as the event rider's killer!

Swimming has a lot to recommend it for those who enjoy it, as you are working against the resistance of the water and using most of the major muscle groups without stressing your joints. There are many other activities which can benefit riders, especially if you can find a teacher who also rides or who understands the demands and needs of a rider. Pilates, which builds core stability and is said to give protection from lower back pain, is especially good, as the techniques translate to finding a centred, balanced position and developing strong abdominal muscles. Yoga will build suppleness, which is an obvious benefit for riders, but recent research has found that it does not really help fitness.

Endurance rider Linda Hams uses skipping as part of her fitness routine.

If you prefer to carry out a specific exercise routine, the following exercises are useful for stretching and mobility. If possible, get an expert such as a chartered physiotherapist or qualified fitness trainer to demonstrate them to you and learn to carry them out under supervision. However, if this is not possible, start gently and take the cautious approach. Remember that it is important to exercise opposing muscle groups, whatever area of the body you are working on. For instance, if you work the quadriceps muscles at the front of the leg, you also need to work the hamstrings at the back.

● The quadriceps stretch. Stand with your weight equally distributed on both feet; bend the right knee, then take hold of the right foot behind you and stretch – gently at first and never to the point of discomfort or pain. Repeat with the left leg.

- The hamstring stretch. Cross one leg in front of the other, close together. Keep the front knee pressed straight against the back knee and bend forward from the hips.

- The Achilles' tendon stretch. Stand on a small step and let your heels hang down until you can feel the stretch.

- The adductor muscles stretch. Stretch your right leg straight out sideways, then bend the left knee until you can feel a stretch on the right leg. Repeat with the left leg.

- The back extension stretch. Lie on your stomach, with your arms bent close to your sides. With your hands on the floor just under your shoulders, push up so that your arms are straight, keeping your pelvis on the floor so that your back is arched.

- The back flexion stretch. Lie on your back and roll up like a ball by bending both knees to your chest and holding your knees. Pull your knees towards you.

Event rider Jo Lawrence finds that training her dogs for agility classes also helps her own fitness.

Pay yourself the same consideration you pay your horse and warm up before you exercise – and before you ride – and cool down afterwards. Getting out of your car and onto your horse after a day's work in an office can lead to aches and pains and pulled muscles, yet many of us do it without thinking. Yet just 5–10 minutes of brisk walking, swinging your arms, will loosen you up before you ride.

Desk-bound riders and people under stress often suffer from tightness across the shoulders and neck. A simple shoulder circling exercise is a good way to prevent this, or to relieve the tension if it's crept up without you realizing. Stand with your feet as far apart as the width of your hips, then slowly circle your shoulders in a backwards rotation; performing 10 shoulder circles twice a day, or at any time you feel tight or tense, will make you feel and ride much better.

Back to basics

Back pain is one of the curses of modern life and is something to which many riders are susceptible. The good news is that riding is not usually the direct cause of a back problem, though it will highlight any problems, which should not be ignored.

Poor posture is the back's biggest enemy, and most of us are at fault. We slump in badly designed chairs, hunch over telephones and contort our spines instead of keeping the vertebrae in three gently curving stacks. The classically correct riding position, where an imaginary perpendicular line passes through the rider's ear, hip and heel is also the best one for your back. However, a saddle that is out of balance and tips you forward or backward can make life uncomfortable for you and your horse – you can't maintain a correct position if you are fighting your saddle.

Everyone who looks after horses also needs to make sure they lift any weights correctly, whether large buckets of water or hay bales. If you are fit and healthy, bending is good for the spine, because it opens the joints and stretches the ligaments. However, bending and lifting together can cause problems.

Rather than struggle with heavy loads, keep them as light as possible by dividing them into smaller ones. Position yourself as close to the load as possible, then bend your knees, keeping your back as straight as possible.

As you lift, pull in your stomach muscles to increase intra-abdominal pressure. If possible, lift in stages, from one level to the next.

When carrying loads, avoid walking in a stooped position and don't hoist heavy hay bales or bags of feed over your shoulder, as stooping causes more pressure on the lower lumbar discs.

The mental approach

Over the past few years, there has been much more focus on the mental approach to riding. Eventing star Pippa Funnel is a high-profile example of someone who has benefited from working with a sports psychologist to overcome competition nerves and many riders and trainers are interested in approaches such as Neuro-Linguistic Programming. They are the subject of many good books and if you're finding that riding is causing as much stress as satisfaction – perhaps because you are finding it difficult to meet your goals, or simply because time management is difficult – investigation could prove dividends.

In basic terms, aim to clear your mind of other areas of your life and accompanying problems before you start caring for or riding your horse. Just the simple act of closing your eyes and taking a few slow, deep breaths before you go to your horse will help. Correct breathing, drawing air down into the diaphragm rather than taking shallow, quick breaths, will help both physically and mentally.

Appendix

Although there are many principles that apply to getting a horse fit, there are also many approaches. Hopefully, this book will help you work out the best approach for you and your horse. However, you may want to find out more information about various topics and the following sources may help.

For more information on TTEAM and TTOUCH in the UK, see www.ttouchtteam.co.uk and www.tilleyfarm.co.uk
For information on these worldwide, see www.tellingtonttouch.com

Clare MacLeod is an independent equine nutritionist who is registered with the Nutrition Society. She has a Masters Degree in human and equine sports science and her particular areas of interest are nutrition for performance in horses and humans and feeding the horse naturally. Her equine clients range from racehorses to companion donkeys: see www.equinenutritionist.co.uk

Other useful websites are:

Association of British Riding Schools www.abrs.org

British Association of Equine Dental Technicians www.equinedentistry.org.uk

British Equine Veterinary Association www.beva.org.uk

British Horse Society www.bhs.org.uk

Farriers Registration Council www.farrier-reg.gov.uk

International League for the Protection of Horses www.ilph.org

Society of Master Saddlers www.mastersaddlers.co.uk

Useful reading

Coumbe, Karen, *First Aid for Horses*, J.A. Allen (London) 2000, ISBN 0 85131 780 4

Diggle, Martin and Raynor, Maggie, *Basic Schooling Made Simple*, J.A. Allen (London) 2002, ISBN 0 85131 843 6

Henderson, Carolyn, *Tack: How to Choose it and Use it*, Swan Hill Press (UK) 1996, ISBN 1 85310 596 1

Henderson, Carolyn and Russell, Lynn, *How to Buy the Right Horse*, Swan Hill Press (UK) 1996, ISBN 1 85310 722 0

Henderson, John, *The Glovebox Guide to Transporting Horses*, J.A. Allen (London) 2005, ISBN 0 85131 878 9

Klimke, Reiner, *Cavalletti*, J.A. Allen (London) 1969, ISBN 15131 192 X (This title was first published in Germany by Franck'sche Verlagshandlung, Kosmos-Verlag, Stuttgart. It has been reprinted several times and revised by the author's daughter, Ingrid. Details for the most recent editions are: Klimke, Ingrid and Reiner, *Cavalletti*, J.A. Allen (London) 2000, ISBN 0 85131 755 3

Lilley, Claire, *Schooling with Ground Poles*, J.A. Allen (London) 2003, ISBN 0 85131 864 9

Lodge, Ray and Shanks, Susan, *All-Weather Surfaces for Horses*, J.A. Allen (London) 2005, ISBN 0 85131 913 0

Loriston-Clarke, Jennie, *Lungeing and Long Reining*, Kenilworth Press (UK) 1993, ISBN 1 87208 214 9

MacLeod, Clare, *The Truth About Feeding Your Horse*, J.A. Allen (London) 2006, ISBN 0 85131 918 1

Marlin, David and Nankervis, Kathryn, *Equine Exercise Physiology*, Blackwell Publishing (UK) 2002, ISBN 0 63205 552 9

Oliver, Robert and Langrish, Bob, *A Photographic Guide to Conformation*, J.A. Allen (London) 2002, ISBN 0 85131 851 7

Warth, Keith, *Stables and Other Equestrian Buildings*, J.A. Allen (London) 1997, ISBN 0 85131 687 5

Index